GEM TRAILS OF ARIZONA

by

Bessie W. Simpson
and
James R. Mitchell

$6.95

Gem Guides Book Company
315 Cloverleaf Dr., Suite F
Baldwin Park, CA 91706

ISBN 935182-42-X

Maps: *Jean Hammond*

Wood from near Winslow

Wood from near St. John

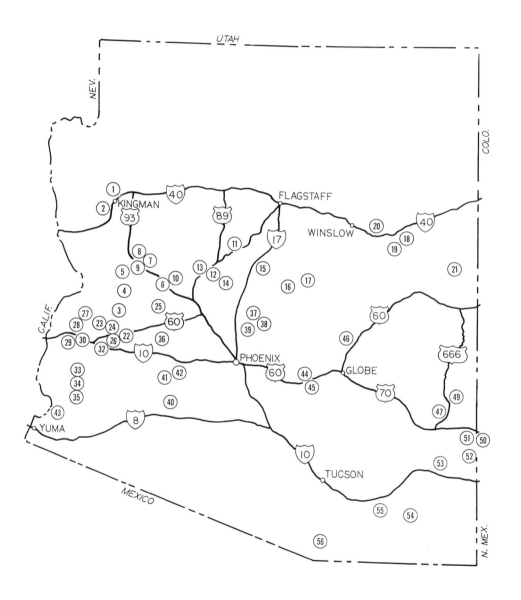

Table of Contents

INTRODUCTION

Arizona is noted for its abundance of minerals and gemstones. Rockhounds come from all over the world to explore this scenic state, searching for its mineral treasures. The supply seems limitless and, best of all, many of the prime collecting sites are situated on public lands.

Each of the locations listed in the revised *Gem Trails of Arizona* was checked shortly before publication to verify mineral availability and that collecting was allowed. A few of the spots are privately owned and a fee is charged. That information is noted in the text.

DO NOT ASSUME THAT THIS GUIDE GIVES PERMISSION TO COLLECT! Land status changes frequently. If you have a suspicion that a particular site is no longer open, be sure to check that status before proceeding. If nothing can be determined locally, land ownership information is available at the County Recorder's office.

Be advised that some of the sites are located on the dumps of old abandoned mines. DO NOT, under any circumstances, enter shafts, and always be cautious when exploring the surrounding regions There are often hidden tunnels, rotted ground and pits, as well as rusty nails, broken glass and discarded chemicals; all of which create a potential hazard.

Most of the areas discussed on the following pages are fairly easy to get to, but road conditions can change. Severe weather can make good roads very rough and rough roads impassable, even with four-wheel drive. Do not attempt traveling where your vehicle was not designed to go.

The sites are situated in landscapes as full of variety as the minerals themselves. The terrain varies from arid deserts to lofty pine covered peaks. Because of these immense differences, do some advance research on the area you plan to visit. Don't take a trip to the desert during the sweltering summer months or to the high mountains during the winter. Doing so could not only result in an unpleasant trip but it could be dangerous.

When venturing into some of the more remote areas it is a good idea to take extra drinking water, foul weather clothing and, possibly, some food, just in case you get delayed or stuck. I am certain that if you take some time to plan your collecting trip properly and make sure your vehicle is in good working order, the gem fields listed on the following pages will provide you and your family with outstanding minerals and many memorable experiences.

WHITE ONYX
Kingman

This site features top quality banded white onyx, most of which is solid and takes a high polish. The material is of such high quality that the Mojave County Gem Stoners Club of Kingman has protected it by a claim. At time of publication, however, amateur collectors are allowed to gather specimens at no charge. If, when you visit, it appears the status may have changed, be sure to inquire locally.

To reach the site from Kingman, take the Stockton Hill Road turnoff (Exit 51) from Interstate 40 and go north ten and one-tenth miles, as shown on the map. As you approach the given mileage, diggings can be seen on the lower slopes of the hill to the left. There are some ruts leading off the main road to the small quarry and most vehicles should have little difficulty getting most of the way. If you have any doubts, simply park off the main road, and hike the short distance.

The best onyx is generally found still in the tough seams, and it takes lots of work to remove sizeable specimens. Gads, chisels, gloves, goggles and heavy hammers are needed to properly work here, but the fine quality of the material makes the work worth it. If you don't feel like doing such labor, there is lots of adequate material lying throughout the dumps and many quality chunks can be gathered in very little time. Most, however, are somewhat small and weathered.

White onyx

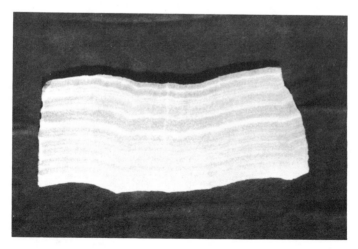

WHITE ONYX
KINGMAN

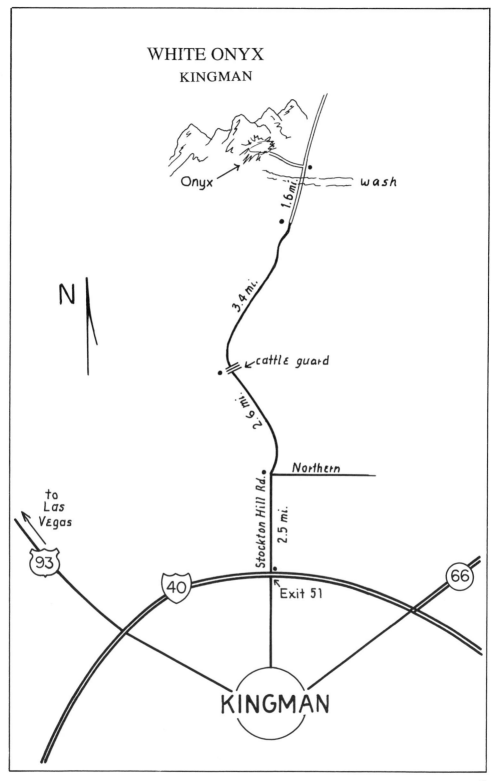

Onyx

wash

1.6 mi.

N

3.4 mi.

cattle guard

2.6 mi.

Northern

Stockton Hill Rd.

to
Las
Vegas

93

40

2.5 mi.

Exit 51

66

KINGMAN

CUESTA FIRE AGATE
Oatman

This is one of Arizona's best known fire agate locations. The claims have been open to collectors willing to pay a small fee for quite a few years, and, at time of publication, the charge is $5.00 per person per day, with no limit on how much can be obtained. All colors of the rainbow can be found here, including a rare, black fire agate. It is suggested that you bring a rock pick, shovel, small screw driver, whisk broom, sledge hammer, 3-4 foot pry bar, spray bottle with water, some small chisels, and a bucket or bag. Be advised that it is not an easy matter to locate the elusive gemstones and lots of perseverance, skill and luck are required to find the best the site has to offer. Overburden is not removed by the owners and collectors are not permitted to use powered equipment or explosives.

Everyone is required to sign a waiver of liability in the event you are hurt while collecting. Specific information about paying the fee and signing the waiver should be obtained in advance by contacting Mrs. Alma Snyder, O.S.R., Box 905, Kingman, AZ 86401. The mine is usually open during the fall, winter and spring, and dry camping is customarily allowed. Limited supplies can be procured in nearby Oatman.

The site is situated just west of Ed's Camp, on Old Highway 66.

Rough fire agate

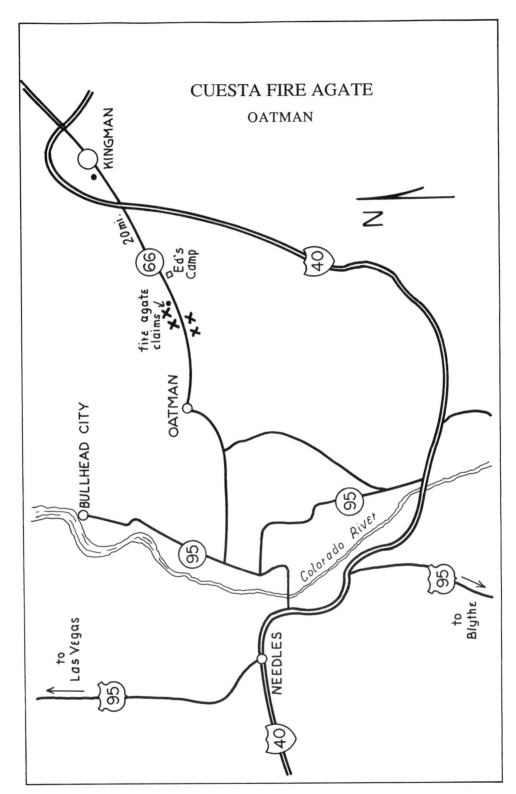

CUESTA FIRE AGATE

OATMAN

DENDRITIC AGATE
AND PALM WOOD BOG

This site features interesting manganese ores, as well as onyx, palm bog and agate. To get there from Wenden, take the Alamo Lake Road twelve and one-half miles and, at that point, continue north onto the dirt pipeline road. Proceed another twelve and nine-tenths miles over the mountains to where ruts can be seen leading east into a wash. Follow them about seven-tenths of a mile and proceed onto the dim road leading to the old manganese mine, four-tenths of a mile further.

Be very careful around the mine, since the tunnel and shafts are rotten and could be very dangerous. In addition, be advised that there are a few mining claims nearby and you shouldn't collect within their boundaries.

Onyx can be found in the canyon about 100 yards north of the mine and is easily spotted, being red and green. Some is delicately banded, while other displays solid colors and patterns. The agate and palm bog litter the higher ground, and some of the palm is opalized, making it especially desirable. Most is found in the grey hills to the south and is picked up from the surface or excavated from the soft soil. The dendritic agate is frequently filled with interesting inclusions, and it takes an excellent polish.

This is a remote collecting area, so be certain your vehicle is in good repair and some extra supplies are on hand in the event you are delayed.

Collecting petrified palm bog and agate

DENDRITIC AGATE AND PALM WOOD BOG

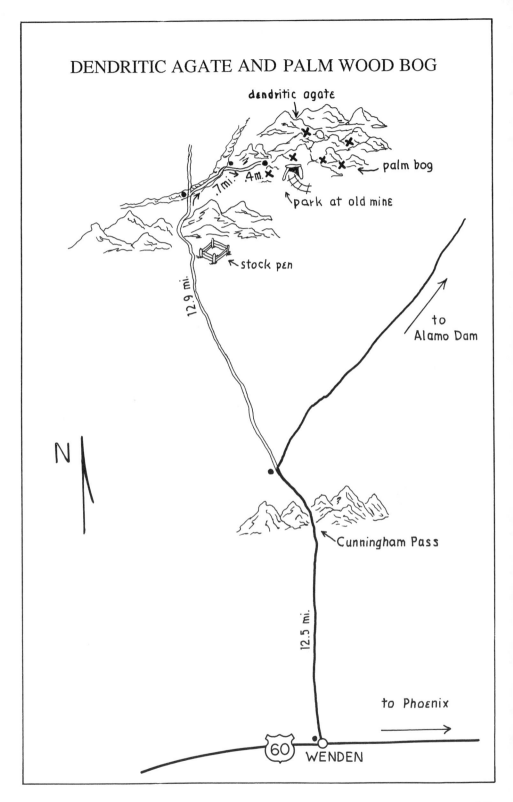

dendritic agate

palm bog

.7mi. 4m.✗

↗park at old mine

←stock pen

12.9 mi.

N

to
Alamo Dam

←Cunningham Pass

12.5 mi.

to Phoenix
→

60 WENDEN

PALM BOG
Alamo Lake

Palm bog is a not-too-common form of palm wood. It was formed from the roots of palm trees growing in marshy areas. Palm bog looks like palm wood with large eyes or spores. It makes very pretty stones and takes a good polish.

This site features petrified wood, palm bog, agate, jasper and rhyolite. To get there, go north from Wenden on the Alamo Lake Road approximately twenty seven and one-half miles. At that point, a dirt road heads off to the right toward the Wayside Inn and you should follow it three and two-tenths miles. From there, turn left, go two and six-tenths miles, and just after crossing the cattle guard, turn right. Continue another five and six-tenths miles and bear right again just before reaching the lake. Drive one more mile and then proceed right up the hill two-tenths of a mile. At the given mileage, the road crosses a light colored clay ridge. This marks the primary collecting site. Roam through the little canyon and search the terrain surrounding the ridge for agate, jasper, banded and swirled rhyolite and petrified wood. Nothing is particularly large here, but most is suitable for producing nice size cabochons. The palm bog makes especially desirable stones, being filled with tiny lines and swirls. The palm is generally tan to brown in color with darker "eyes" or spores.

This entire region is covered with petrified wood, palm and agate, and randomly searching just about anywhere should be fruitful. Be certain, however, not to collect within the boundaries of Alamo Lake State Park, since rockhounding is not allowed in any Arizona State Park. Be also advised that there are lots of rattlesnakes in the area, so always be on the lookout for them.

Palm wood

PALM BOG
ALAMO LAKE

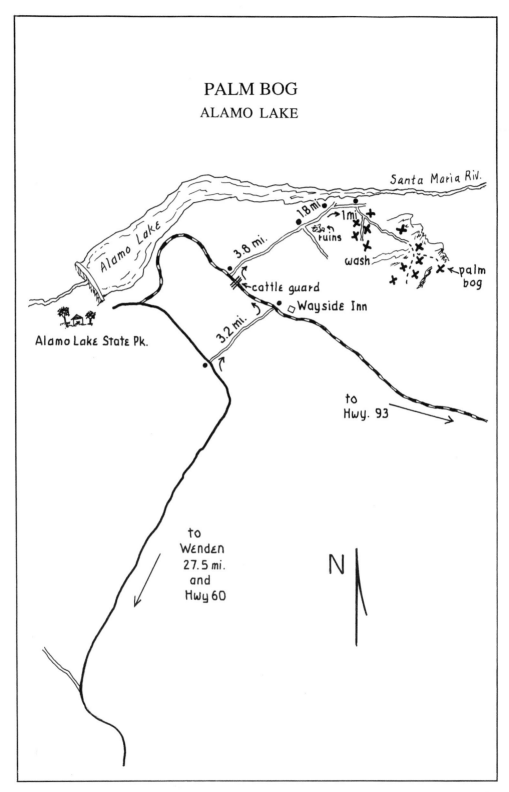

Santa Maria Riv.

Alamo Lake

.18 mi.

1 mi.

ruins

wash

3.8 mi.

cattle guard

palm bog

Alamo Lake State Pk.

Wayside Inn

3.2 mi.

to Hwy. 93

to Wenden 27.5 mi. and Hwy 60

N

WOOD
Signal

Outstanding specimens of chert, agate, jasper, feldspar, mica, petrified wood and petrified palm can be found in the three extensive sites illustrated on the accompanying map. To get to Site A, go west on Signal Road which intersects Highway 93 eight and three-tenths miles south of Wikieup. The dirt road is well graded, and shouldn't present a problem for most vehicles. After having gone seventeen and one-half miles, turn left and proceed four and two-tenths miles to where a sandy wash intersects from the east. If you have four-wheel drive, follow the sandy wash about seven-tenths of a mile. On the cliffs to the south, at the given mileage, one can find pink feldspar, often associated with delicate books of mica, some of which makes excellent display pieces for a mineral collection.

Another one and six-tenths miles along the main road is Site B. This site features a wide variety of collectables, including colorful jasper, chert and petrified wood. Simply roam the slopes on both sides of the road, keeping a keen eye to the ground. Specimens don't tend to be very large, but the quality more than makes up for that deficiency.

The most productive of all three sites is the vast region labeled Site C. Simply park anywhere within the area and look for agate, jasper, petrified wood and petrified palm. Some specimens are sizeable, and most is of top quality, capable of taking a high polish.

Needless to say, this is a very remote collecting location, and it is imperative that your vehicle is in good repair before visiting.

Collecting petrified wood

16

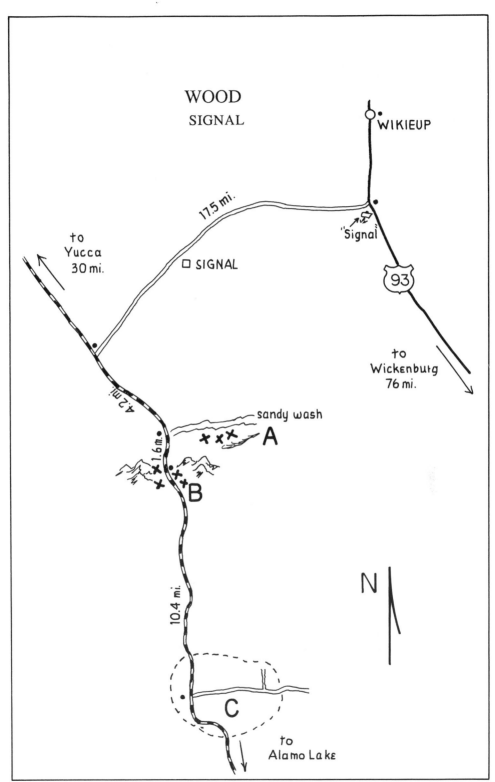

WOOD
SIGNAL

WIKIEUP

to
Yucca
30 mi.

17.5 mi.

□ SIGNAL

"Signal"

93

to
Wickenburg
76 mi.

4.2 mi.

1.6 m.

sandy wash

× × ×   A

× × ×
×   B

10.4 mi.

N

C

to
Alamo Lake

DESERT ROSES

This site is easy to get to and most vehicles should be able to make it with no problem. To get there, simply go four and one-tenth miles north on Highway 93 from where it crosses over Highway 71. At that point, Alamo Road intersects from the left, and there is a stop sign just off the pavement to help identify the road. Proceed west on the well graded dirt road five and eight-tenths miles to where some ruts will be seen leading off to the north. Follow those ruts about eight-tenths of a mile, turn right, go a short distance and park. This area has long been known by collectors, and, in spite of its size, much of the prime surface material has been picked up. It seems, though, that after every rainstorm, a new crop of the delicate chalcedony roses are exposed.

If you have time, the best way to find well formed specimens is to hike away from the roads. Pay particularly close attention to washes and other areas of erosion in the region shown on the map as well as throughout the foothills of nearby Fire Mountain and the surrounding flatlands.

The chalcedony is easy to spot, since its bright white color stands out vividly against the darker soil. This is especially true after a recent rainstorm. Randomly roaming throughout the brush, keeping your eyes to the ground, is the best way to search.

Supplies are available in Congress, Aguila and Wickenburg.

Desert roses

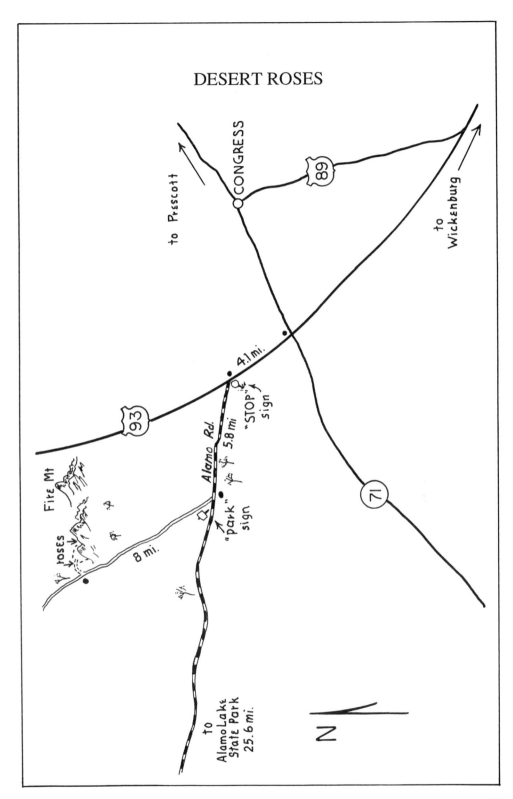

DESERT ROSES

PASTELITE
Near Bagdad

The region surrounding Burro Creek is well known among rockhounds for the wide variety of cutting material that can be obtained there. To get to this renowned site from Highway 93, proceed to the tiny town of Nothing, Arizona, or turn right onto Highway 97 and go two and one-half miles. At that point, proceed left onto the dirt road leading over the hill approximately seven miles. At the given mileage, you should be at Burro Creek and the collecting is done throughout the hills and flatlands on both sides of the river, as shown on the map. The dirt road to the creek isn't bad and most rugged vehicles shouldn't have difficulty making the trip.

The pastelite is not hard to find due to its colorful nature and plentiful supply. If willing to spend time exploring the area, you should be able to procure a good quantity, some in delicate shades of pink, orange, brown and a variety of mixed colors. If not satisfied with what can be found scattered throughout the lowlands, you can attack any of the numerous seams in an effort to obtain additional specimens. This is tough work, but the rewards often make it worthwhile. You will need a sledge hammer, chisels, gads, pry bar, gloves and goggles if you do attack the seams, so be prepared.

If you plan to spend a few days here, there is a nice campground only a short distance from the pastelite area.

Pastelite collecting area

PASTELITE-NEAR
BAGDAD

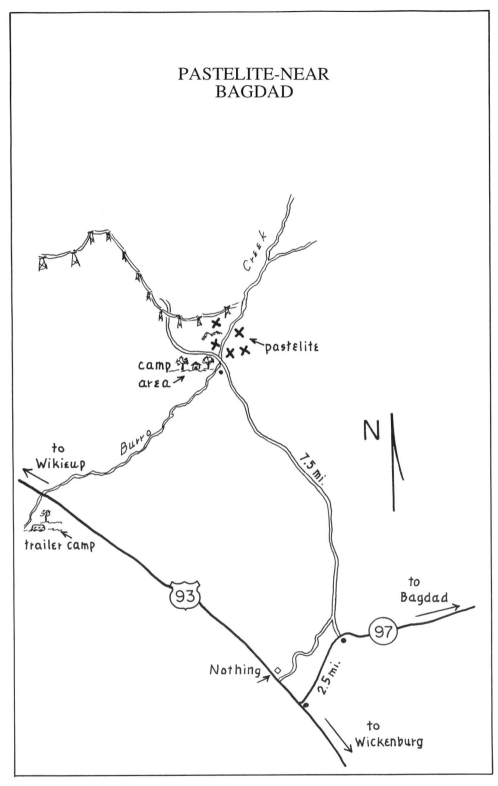

DENDRITIC OPALIZED BENTONITE

To get to Site A, follow the ruts leading from the main road a short distance and park. All along the road, especially near the hillsides, one can find lots of top quality agate, opalite and pastelite. A few digging areas will be seen, and it is generally worthwhile to do a little work there, if you feel up to tackling the seams with sledge, gads and chisels.

One and one-half miles further along the main road is a white bank that designates Site B. Colorful opalized bentonite can be found about three to four feet deep in the white clay, sometimes being covered with white or green opalite. This is a prime area of interest at Burro Creek, but be willing to do some tough digging to obtain worthwhile quantities.

Additional collecting can be done by returning to the highway access road, crossing Burro Creek and going approximately eight-tenths of a mile. At that point, pastelite, opalite and occasional chunks of jasper and agate will be found scattered all over. Take the tracks leading to the west about three-tenths of a mile toward the obvious white outcrop where tons of white and grey pastelite can be procured, some being filled with interesting inclusions. This is labeled Site C on the map.

Continue north along the main road another seven-tenths of a mile to the power lines and explore the surrounding terrain. This locality boasts pink, orange, white and grey pastelite, opalite and agate. A gas line road is intersected four-tenths of a mile further north and more material can be found at that intersection. The best is procured, however, by proceeding four-tenths of a mile west along the pipeline road, turning left and continuing another one-tenth of mile to where the ground is covered with colorful agate and jasper, as well as light green, orange, grey and white pastelite. This is Site D.

Searching for agate and pastelite

DENDRITIC OPALIZED
BENTONITE

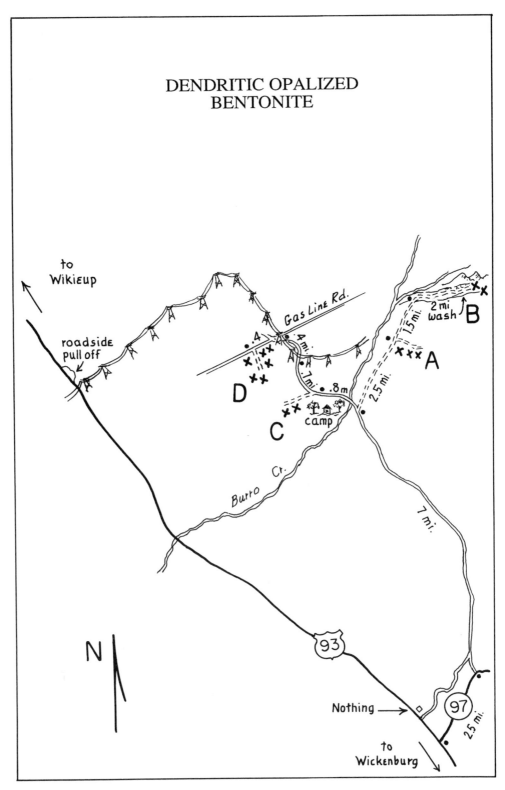

to
Wikieup

roadside
pull off

Gas Line Rd.

.4   .4 mi.

1.5 mi.

2 mi.
wash   B

X X

D   X X X   A

.7 mi.   .8 m   2.5 mi.

X X   camp

C   X X

Burro   Cr.

7 mi.

N

93

Nothing   97

2.5 mi.

to
Wickenburg

APACHE TEARS
Burro Creek

The Apache tears found at this site are a little different than those obtained at other locations. Here, the stones do not sparkle in the sunlight, looking something like small chunks of charcoal. For that reason, walk away from the sun, not toward it, as you usually do when collecting Apache tears. By searching in this manner, the tears will look like dark black pebbles in the lighter colored soil and thereby be easy to spot.

Two types of Apache tears can be found. They appear identical on the surface, but tumbling to remove the crust will reveal that some are opaque and others are beautifully banded. The banded stones exhibit light and dark areas and a few will even produce a chatoyant or cat's-eye effect. The opaque variety may be substituted for jet black onyx, or cut thin and used for backing material in opal doublets.

To get to this Apache tear location, follow Highway 93 north about 59 miles from Wickenburg to the large bridge spanning Burro Creek. The tears are scattered all over on both sides of the river for quite a distance, but the greatest concentration seems to be on the flat mesa and its lower slopes situated about one-half mile south of the bridge.

There is a nice B.L.M. campground next to the river, as shown on the map, and it can serve as a pleasant base for Burro Creek rockhounding if you plan to spend a few days.

Apache tears

APACHE TEARS
BURRO CREEK

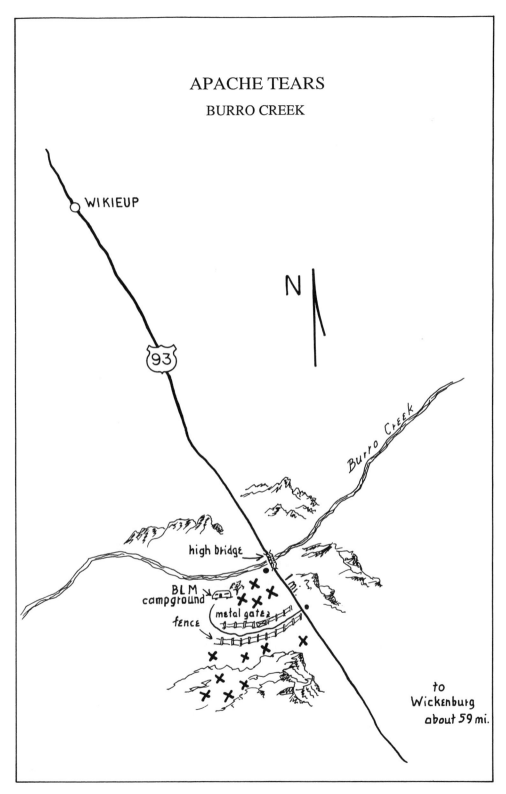

WIKIEUP

93

N

Burro Creek

high bridge

1 mi.

BLM
campground

metal gates

fence

to
Wickenburg
about 59 mi.

QUARTZ CRYSTALS
Date Creek

This is not a new hunting area but it is one that is easy to get to and seems to pay off every time. In fact, just about every rainstorm unearths a new supply of beautiful quartz crystals.

The turnoff is one and three-tenths miles north of where Alamo Road intersects Highway 93, as shown on the map. There is a sign designating "Date Creek Ranch Road" and it is there that you should turn east. Follow the graded dirt road about two and one-half miles to the edge of the Date Creek Mountains. At that point, there will be some ruts to the right which should be followed only a short distance further to where signs of previous campfires can be seen, those marking the parking area.

Pull off the road and examine all terrain from the campfire rings toward the mountains. As you proceed, numerous pits will be spotted, designating where previous collectors have dug for the crystals. Single crystals and clusters can be found here, and the best seem to be obtained by doing some digging. Use existing pits for indications as to where to start your own excavations. Some nice scepter crystals are said to have come from this renowned location, but they are few and far between. Maybe you will be lucky enough to find some. There is also lots of bright white milky quartz scattered all over the hillsides which might be of interest for use in landscaping.

Clear quartz crystals

QUARTZ CRYSTALS
DATE CREEK

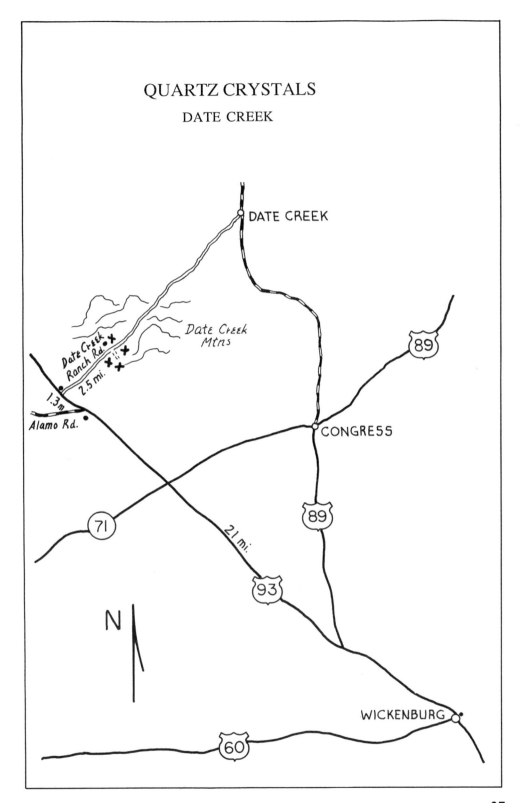

AGATE
Perkinsville

Some of the finest agate in all of central Arizona can be found in the hills and valleys surrounding Perkinsville. To get to the prime collecting region, go south on the Jerome Road from where it intersects the Chino Valley Road, as shown on the map. After having gone about six and one-half miles you will be in the center of this well respected rockhounding area. From there, extending quite a distance in all directions, the hills are filled with colorful agate. It seems that the largest pieces are generally found in the region between the telephone lines and the cattle guard, but don't neglect other spots along the road.

Perkinsville agate displays a variety of colors and patterns with the most highly prized being the delicate pink material, sometimes being filled with interesting inclusions. Fine multicolored banded agate can also be obtained and it, too, is a real prize.

Be advised that there is lots of private ranchland in this part of Arizona, and you should not enter, without first getting permission to do so. The hills are full of agate. If you have the time, it might be fruitful to obtain consent to explore some of the private lands, especially if not satisfied with what can be picked up near the road and on open areas.

It is recommended, while in the area, that you continue to the ghost town of Jerome. Jerome was a copper mining town boasting over 15,000 people and is situated on a steep side of Cleopatra Hill. The scenic old city is now restored and accommodates many shops and a fascinating mining museum, all of which should make the trip worth the time.

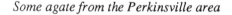

Some agate from the Perkinsville area

AGATE

PERKINSVILLE

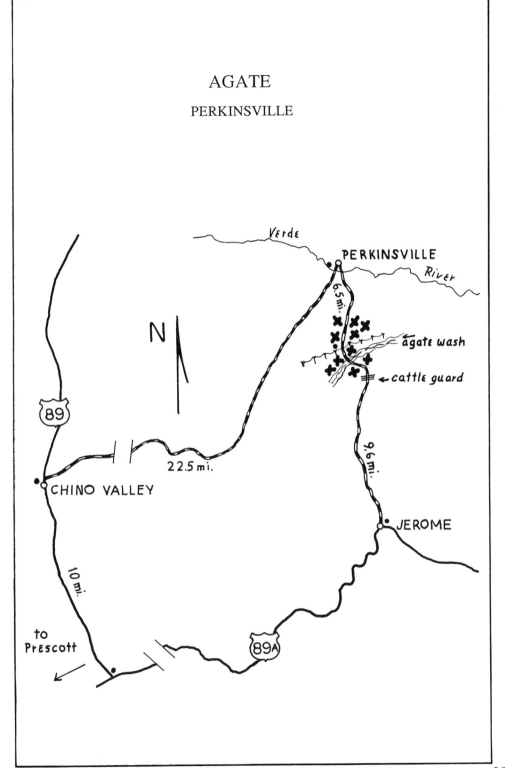

MINERALS
Prescott

In the middle of the nineteenth century gold was discovered in the Bradshaw Mountains near the present site of Prescott. In the ensuing years, countless mines shafts were dug into the mountains and their associated dumps can still be seen scattered throughout the landscape. These dumps often contain a wide variety of outstanding mineral specimens which include iron pyrite, chalcopyrite, numerous copper ores, galena, hematite, sphalerite, quartz, calcite and countless other minerals. The pyrite is often especially nice since it sometimes occurs in bright white quartz giving the appearance of gold. Be advised that some of the dumps are part of currently operating and/or privately owned mines, and should therefore not be explored. The majority, however, are abandoned and thereby open to collecting.

The accompanying map shows a few of the more productive mine dumps in the region, all of which can provide the collector with an opportunity for finding mineral specimens. Just plan to take some time rummaging through the dumps and splitting any suspect stone to properly ascertain exactly what minerals are hidden by its discolored and weathered surface. Frequently, you will split an otherwise common stone and find it to be filled with sparkling metallic crystals.

Be sure to wear goggles when cracking rocks, do not enter any shafts, and DO NOT TRESPASS onto any privately owned mine dumps. Those illustrated on the accompanying map were accessible at the time of publication, but land status, especially in regard to gold mines, changes rapidly. If there is any doubt, move on and collect elsewhere.

Panning for gold in one of the streams south of Prescott

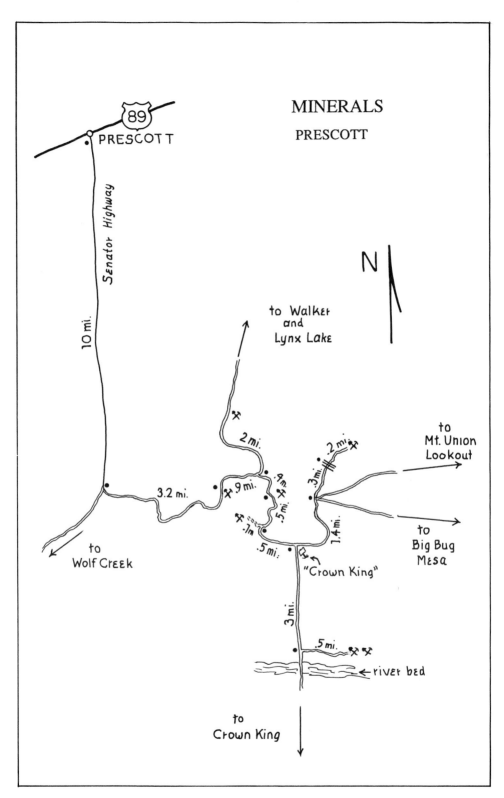

MINERALS
PRESCOTT

MINERALS
Copper Basin

Copper Basin offers rockhounds the opportunity to gather a number of prized minerals, including beautiful blue azurite, green malachite, cuprite, molybdenite, quartz crystals and even gold.

The entire region is PRIVATELY OWNED by the Phelps Dodge Company, and consent must be granted before you pick up anything. Permission generally can be obtained either directly through the company or with the on-site caretaker. It should be noted that collecting status changes from time to time depending upon what type mining is taking place, so advance inquiry is recommended. No fee is charged, but rockhounds are restricted to specific areas and a liability release must be signed. If you don't make advance arrangements, it will be necessary to find the caretaker, and this can take some time depending upon where he might be.

Copper Basin provides an easy place to search, since most of the minerals are brightly colored, making them stand out against the native rock like neon lights. Most of what can be picked up, however, is somewhat porous and takes only a fair polish. Be sure to take time to look for the most solid and thick specimens. Pieces with both azurite and malachite are especially desirable and make real prizes in a mineral collection or when polished.

Camping is not allowed on the Phelps Dodge property, but there are lots of side roads in the area which afford good spots to set up for the night.

The road leading to the caretaker's house

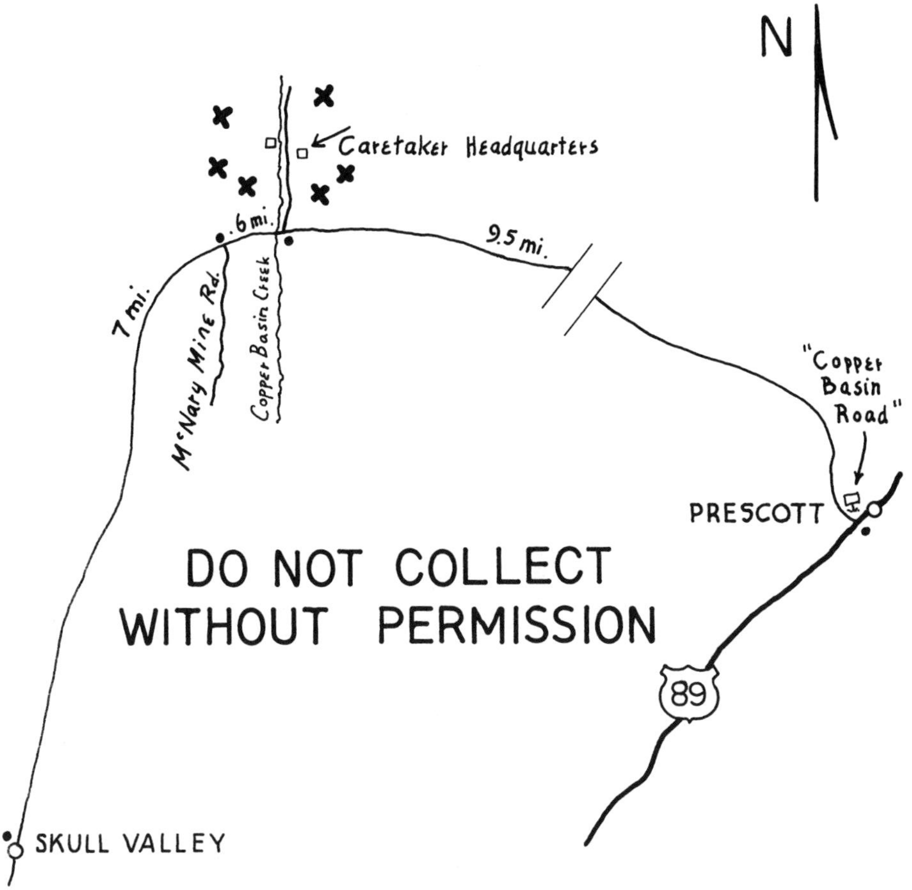

MINERALS

Caretaker Headquarters

N

.6 mi.

9.5 mi.

7 mi.

McNary Mine Rd.

Copper Basin Creek

"Copper Basin Road"

PRESCOTT

DO NOT COLLECT
WITHOUT PERMISSION

89

SKULL VALLEY

ONYX
Mayer

This site features some of the most colorful onyx to be found in all of Arizona and, as unbelievable as it might seem, is situated just off a busy highway. To get there, simply take Highway 69 about 26 miles south from Prescott to the Mayer turnoff, as shown on the map. Continue south one-half mile from the Mayer sign and you will spot a little turnout (not large enough for group parking) to the east. Be prepared to turn as you approach the given mileage, since it is easy to pass the site and this is a very hazardous place to attempt making a "U turn". Pull onto the turnout, park, and then crawl under the highway fence. The onyx is just on the other side, and it isn't difficult to get under the gate.

Specimen size ranges from very large, unmovable boulders to small and easily collected chunks. The onyx is everywhere and it takes discretion to decide what to leave behind and what to take. Careful scrutiny is necessary to sort the best from the not-so-good. Some has nice colorful bands and is very solid, while other pieces contain cavities and/or lack good coloration. The onyx comes in a variety of hues, concentrating on browns, yellows, reds and whites, and is very colorful.

There aren't many camping spots in the immediate vicinity, but there are countless areas in the nearby Prescott National Forest. There, you will be able to camp amongst the tall pines and, if desired, even pan for gold.

Examining a large onyx boulder at the Mayer site

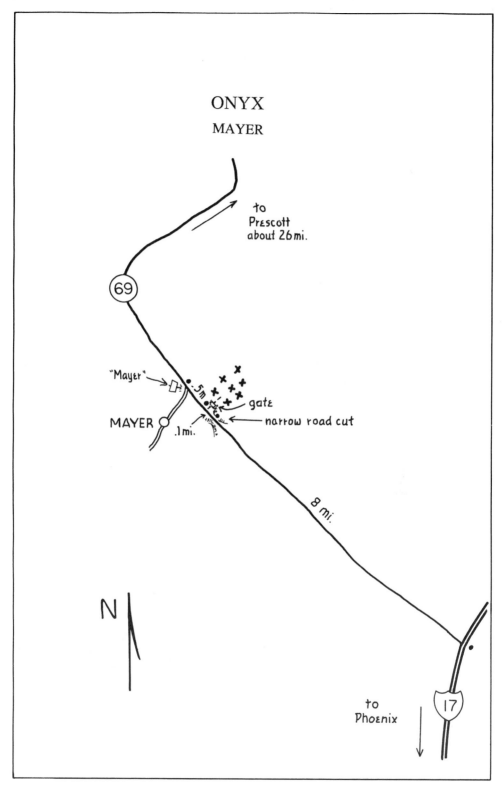

ONYX

MAYER

35

AGATE
Camp Verde Salt Mine

The old salt mine, west of Camp Verde has long been known among Arizona rockhounds. Excellent crystalized specimens of halite, glauberite, gypsum, calcite, aragonite and kyanite can be found there, as well as a host of lesser known minerals.

To get to this fascinating and productive location from Camp Verde, head south out of town about four-tenths of a mile to Salt Mine Road and turn right. Continue one and one-half miles and, as you proceed, a brilliant white hill will be spotted in the west marking the salt mine. As you drive past the hill, there is a little road leading toward it which should be followed to the gate only a short distance away. At that point, park and hike into the salt area. This site is privately owned, but town officials advise that collectors are allowed onto the property as long as they take only a limited number of specimens and do not enter any of the dangerous shafts,

Be sure to wear sun glasses, since the glare from the white salt is blinding on a sunny day. In addition, be very careful when digging into the hill, since it is very easy to damage the delicate crystals with a carelessly placed shovel or pick. Hand tools are much more appropriate here. Look for crystals growing out of the soil and carefully dig them out. Some will exhibit a combination of selenite and glauberite, making outstanding additions to a mineral collection.

Colorful agate can be found at Brown Springs, as illustrated on the map, but the road is very rough. If you decide to make the trip, be sure your vehicle is capable of such a journey and take along some extra supplies in the event you are delayed.

The large pile of salt marking the collecting area

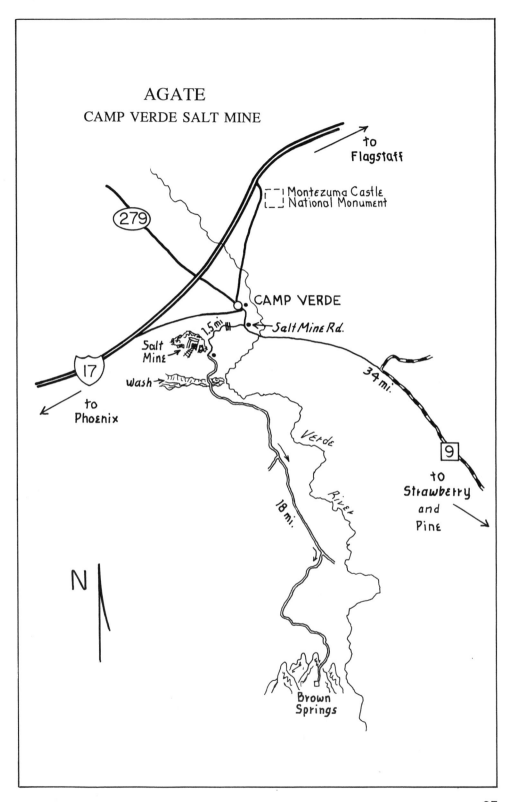

AGATE
CAMP VERDE SALT MINE

to Flagstaff

279

Montezuma Castle
National Monument

CAMP VERDE

Salt Mine Rd.

1.5 mi.

Salt Mine

34 mi.

17

Wash

to Phoenix

Verde

River

9

to Strawberry and Pine

18 mi.

N

Brown Springs

GEODES AND CONCRETIONS
Payson

Site A is one of the best places in Arizona to find geodes. To get there, take Forest Road 64 west from Star Valley Road about 12 miles, as shown on the map. This is a well graded road and should not present difficulty to most vehicles. If you reach a bridge crossing the little creek, you have gone too far and should double back exactly one mile.

The unusual little orbs are found just lying on the surface, and all you must do is carefully scrutinize the terrain on either side of the road. On the south, there is a two rut road about 100 yards up the hill that is virtually paved with geodes and nodules. Inspect ravines, hillsides and areas of erosion or rake through the pine needles to expose otherwise hidden specimens. Digging isn't really necessary, but a small shovel or pick would be helpful for removing geodes that have become partially embedded in the soil.

Size varies greatly, ranging from those as small as peas to others over ten inches in diameter. The small ones are abundant, but grapefruit size specimens are also somewhat easy to find. For the most part, they have bubbly tan exteriors, but some are brown or black. Be advised that a large percentage of the Payson geodes do not contain crystal filled cavities, but they do make nice display pieces uncut. In addition to the geodes, Site A offers nice blue and white agate, so be sure to also keep an eye out for that fine cutting material.

Site B boasts pastel agate, chert and unusual limestone concretions. To get there, take West Main Street, which turns into Country Club Road, four and eight-tenths miles. At the proper mileage, there is a partially obscured road that heads off to the left and you should follow it one mile. Material is found scattered throughout the terrain, on both sides of the road, for at least another mile.

Some geodes from the Payson site

GEODES AND CONCRETIONS
PAYSON

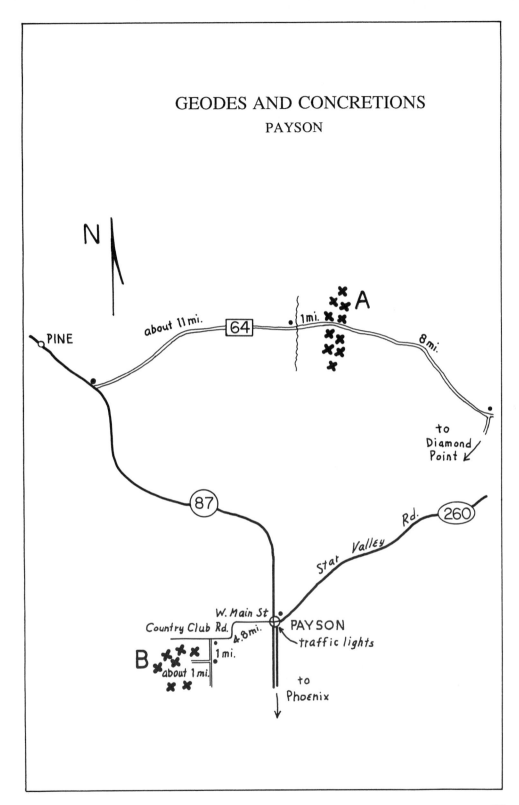

N

PINE

about 11 mi. 64 1 mi. A

8 mi.

to
Diamond
Point

87

Star Valley Rd. 260

W. Main St PAYSON
Country Club Rd. 4.8 mi. traffic lights

B 1 mi.
about 1 mi.

to
Phoenix

QUARTZ CRYSTALS
Diamond Point

This is good hunting area for the summer, when it is hot in the desert. The quartz crystals found at Diamond Point are frequently very clear and many are doubly terminated, often resembling New York's highly prized Herkimer diamonds.

To reach the area, follow Star Valley road from Payson about 14 miles to Forest Road 64. This is a National Forest access road and is well maintained. Go west about four miles and then turn south onto Forest Road 65 approximately three and seven-tenths miles. At that point, pull off the road and park

This spot has been known for years and, for that reason, most of the surface crystals have been picked up. Heavy rainstorms, however, never fail to expose additional specimens on or near the road for quite a distance in all directions. Productive pockets can also be found by hiking from where you park toward the fence overlooking the cliff. You will see where previous rockhounds have worked and, with a little chipping, sifting and digging, you should have no trouble exposing some of these tiny but perfect little gems.

Generally, the most productive method for locating the elusive crystals is to work with gads, chisels and hammers on the many boulders strewn throughout the area. This is hard work, but the rewards are usually worth it. If you don't feel like engaging in such tough labor, try some shallow digging and sifting of the loose soil near the white and orange quartz outcrops. It takes patience to find Diamond Point crystals, but their quality makes the effort worthwhile.

Crystals from Diamond Point

QUARTZ CRYSTALS
DIAMOND POINT

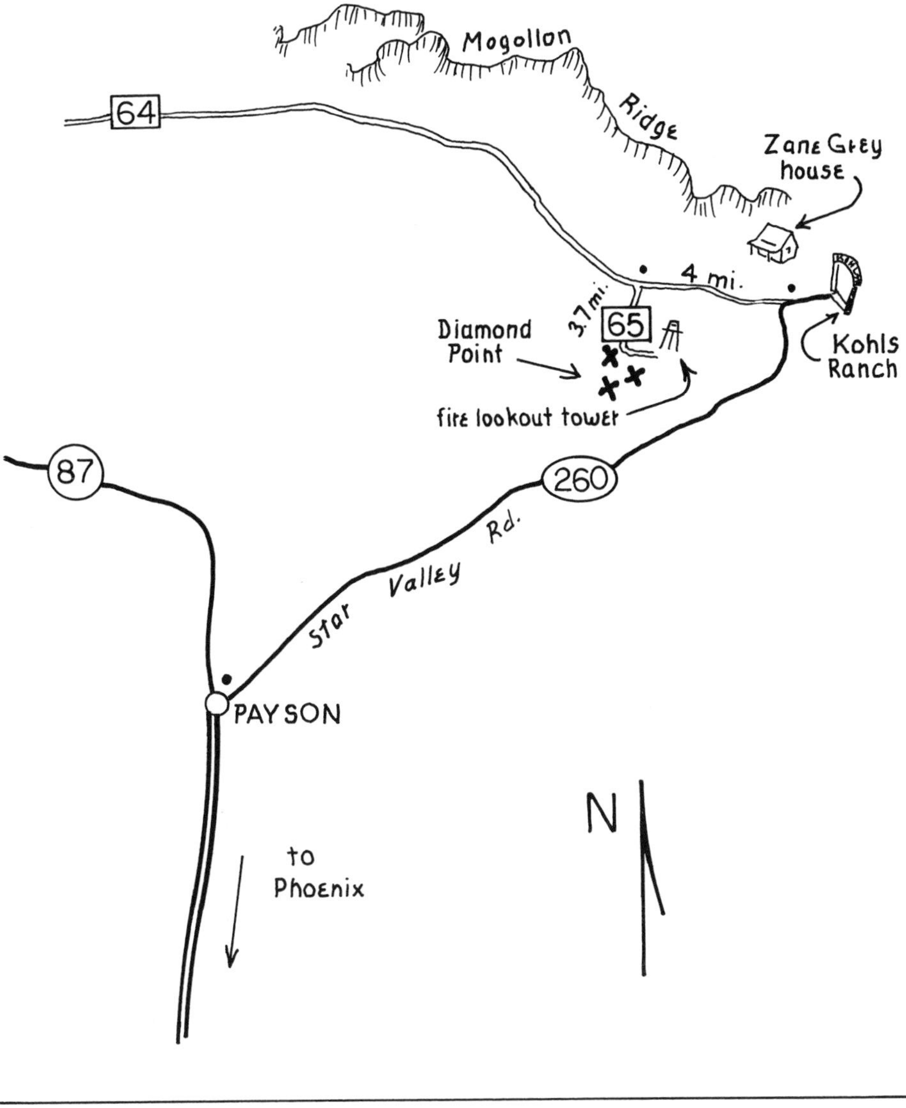

Mogollon

Ridge

64

Zane Grey
house

4 mi.

.37 mi.

65

Diamond
Point

Kohls
Ranch

fire lookout tower

87

260

Star Valley Rd.

PAYSON

to
Phoenix

N

PETRIFIED WOOD
Holbrook

Some of the most beautiful petrified wood in the entire world comes from a limited area near the town of Holbrook. If you would like to gather specimens of this prized material, similar to that found within the protected boundaries of Petrified Forest National Park, there are only a few places where it can be done. One such spot is Patton and Sons, a fee location situated near the southern entrance of the park. To get there from Holbrook, take Highway 180 eighteen miles east to the turnoff to Petrified Forest National Park. Turn, and on your left will be a museum and souvenir shop. That is where you must register, receive detailed collecting information, and pay the fee.

Rockhounds pay only $.50 per pound for all wood collected, with a minimum being set at 25 pounds. That minimum is required in order to restrict entry to people who are genuinely interested in gathering petrified wood and not just wanting to do some off road driving throughout the ranch. If you pick up more than you want, it isn't necessary to take it all and if you do not quite get 25 pounds, you can obtain the balance at the store.

Camping is allowed on property near the shop, and there is a graveled area upon which you can park a trailer or motorhome. There is no charge to stay there, but facilities and supplies are very limited. Rest rooms are available during business hours, but water must be self provided.

Collecting wood near the Patton and Sons shop

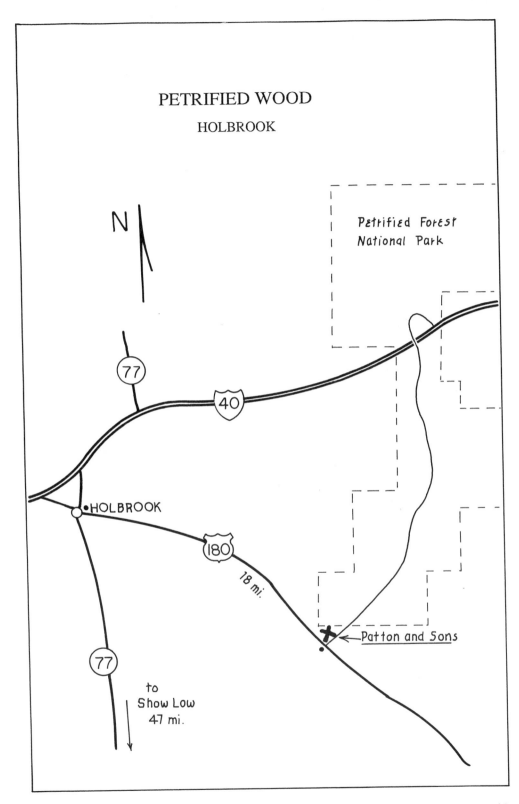

PETRIFIED WOOD

HOLBROOK

N

Petrified Forest
National Park

77

40

77

•HOLBROOK

180

18 mi.

Patton and Sons

to
Show Low
47 mi.

COLORFUL PETRIFIED WOOD
Woodruff Area

If you would like to gather specimens of petrified wood similar to that protected within the boundaries of Petrified Forest National Park, there is a fine place to do so a short distance south of Holbrook, near the small town of Woodruff. Most of what can be found is not too large, but great for making cabochons and for tumbling.

To get there, take Highway 77 south from Holbrook about six and one-half miles and then turn left toward Woodruff. From that point, heading east all the way to Silver Creek on both sides of the road, one can pick up pieces of the spectacularly colored wood. The most prolific concentration, however, is about three to four miles from Highway 77. There, chunks of the highly prized material are scattered everywhere. There is a little hill, on the south side of the road, three and one-half miles from Highway 77 which provides a good place from which to base your search.

Size tends to be small, but there are a few larger specimens scattered about. In addition, one can find an occasional perfectly formed twig. This material is of the highest quality, and takes an outstanding polish. Colors include bright yellow, orange, red and white.

The area stretching about 20 miles south of Woodruff along the ranch road following Silver Creek is also a good hunting area. Be sure, however, to check for loose sand before pulling off any roads in this area.

While collecting near Woodruff, be on the lookout for agate also, especially a fine variety of moss agate.

Collecting along the little road about 3 1/2 miles from Highway 77

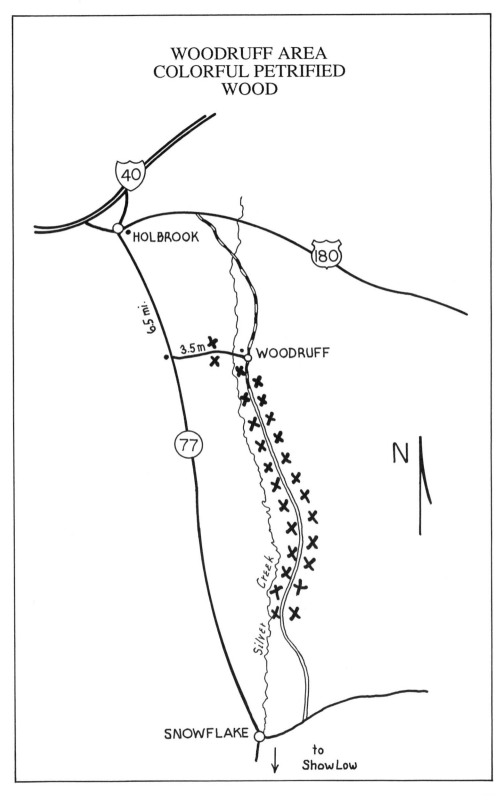

WOODRUFF AREA
COLORFUL PETRIFIED WOOD

40

HOLBROOK

180

6.5 mi.

3.5 m

WOODRUFF

77

N

Silver Creek

SNOWFLAKE

to Show Low

WOOD
Near Joseph City

Some often sizeable specimens of petrified wood can be found in the hills just east of Joseph City. One of the most prolific areas is reached by taking Exit 277 from Interstate 40 and bearing right three-tenths of a mile. At that point, there will be a power line road which you should follow north one-half mile and then turn right to the top of the little hill, about one-tenth of a mile further.

From the moment you step out of your vehicle, you will see petrified wood littering the hills. Hike into the valley, and huge stumps will be observed. Most of the wood is not as colorful as that found near Holbrook and Woodruff, occurring, for the most part, in shades of grey. There are some colorful pieces to be found, though, but generally in solid tones. Some of the best is a brilliant yellow material with vivid red stringers. Much of what can be found here is crumbly, so be selective.

Some of the stumps weigh many tons, being virtually impossible to remove. In addition, remember that the government restricts quantities of petrified wood that any single person can take from public lands. Those regulations state that the maximum amount one can obtain per day is 25 pounds, plus one piece, provided that the maximum total for one calendar year does not exceed 250 pounds.

In addition to the wood, this site boasts nice agate, displaying a variety of color and pattern combinations.

A shattered petrified log near Joseph City

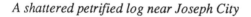

WOOD NEAR
JOSEPH CITY

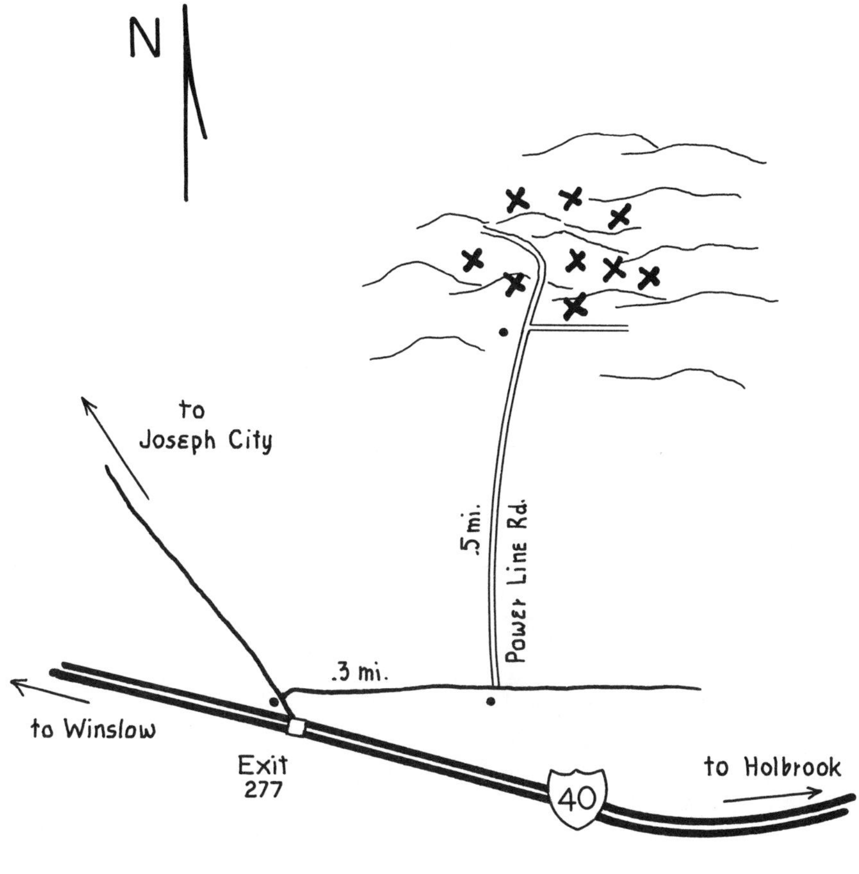

N

to
Joseph City

.5 mi.

Power Line Rd.

.3 mi.

to Winslow

Exit
277

to Holbrook

40

FLOWER AGATE
St. Johns

This site, at time of publication, is temporarily CLOSED and mentioned only in hopes that it will reopen at a later date. The location features some of Arizona's most interesting agate which has been named "flower agate" by collectors who have admired its incredible beauty. The prime material consists of a beautiful white or blue background with colorful dendritic patterns, some showing black plumes and vivid flower designs. The agate is obtained on land leased by Mr. Richey, in St. Johns, and, at the present time, he is having some difficulty retaining rights to the access road.

Collectors can see or purchase some of this fine material at the Richey shop which is reached by going two streets west of the court house to the road leading to the dump. From there, proceed a short distance to his shop, which is easily identified by its grey siding and a gate with a blue sign designating it to be the Richey home. For current information, he can be reached by writing to 2nd west 6th North St, St Johns, Arizona 85936 or by calling (602) 337-4596.

If restrictions are eliminated when you plan to visit, it is a good idea to make advance collecting arrangements with Mr. Richey, and it is essential that you have a rugged vehicle designed to traverse rough roads. Mr. Richey should be able advise you in regard to road conditions and other pertinent information when you visit.

FLOWER AGATE

ST. JOHNS

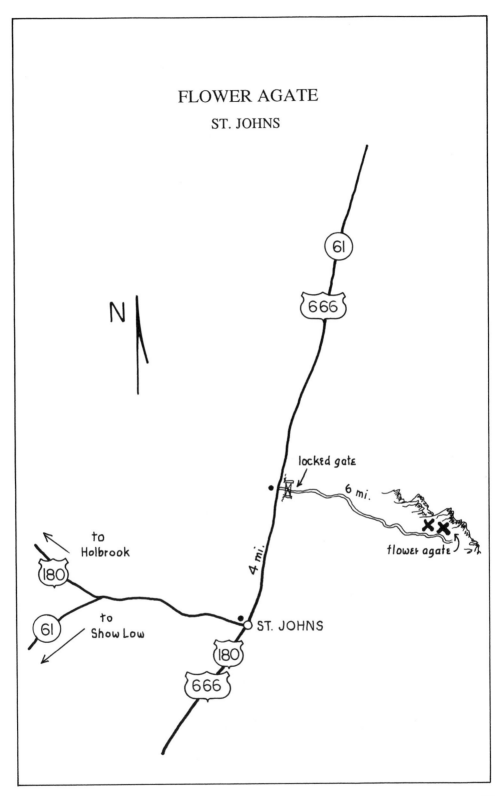

HARQUAHALA MINE

Not far from Salome rests the remains of the once booming town of Harquahala. Remnants of the mining operation and a number of the town's old buildings can still be visited. In addition, there are some nice mineral specimens available to the rockhound who is willing to spend some time digging through the dumps and rock piles.

The town began with the discovery of gold in 1888 by Harry Watton, Bob Stein and Mike Sullivan. Before the ore ran out, the total production was about $2,500,000. On the dumps, collectors can find fine specimens of red hematite, quartz, chrysocolla, malachite, dioptase, calcite, pyrite, chalcopyrite, galena and even some delicate gypsum.

To get there, take Highway 60 to Salome and then head south on the Harquahala Mine Road about 12 miles. The dumps are easily spotted on the hills, and the remnants of the town can be reached by driving to the base of the mountain. The road is not a bad dirt road, but it is rough in places.

If you do decide to explore the dumps of this interesting townsite, be sure to drive carefully, keeping in mind that this is a desert and can get very hot during the summer. When near the mines, be very careful, since there are lots of rusty nails and some broken glass. In addition, DO NOT ENTER ANY MINE SHAFTS!

Another region of productive mine dumps is located 4.2 miles north of nearby Wenden, as shown on the map. You can find nice pyrite and other mineral specimens on those dumps.

Minerals from the Harquahala Mine

HARQUAHALA MINE MINERALS

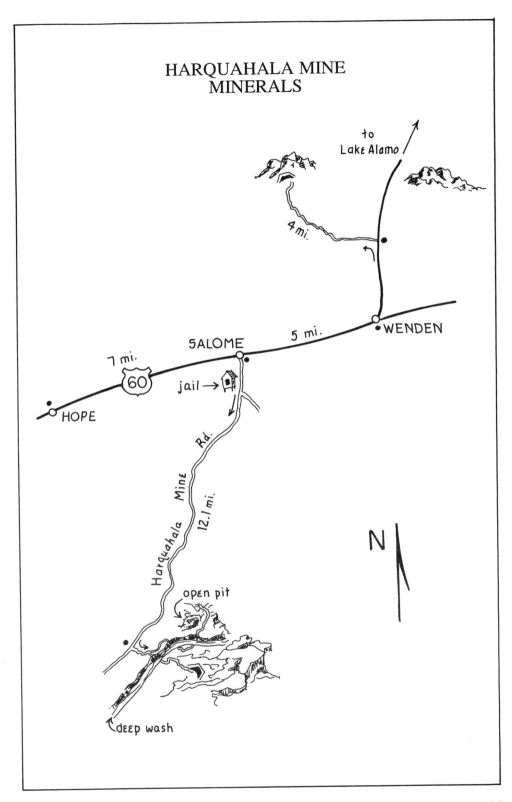

to Lake Alamo

4 mi.

5 mi. WENDEN

SALOME

7 mi.
60

jail →

HOPE

Harquahala Mine Rd.

12.1 mi.

N

open pit

deep wash

PLOMOSA MOUNTAINS

This site features agate and jasper in a wide variety of colors and patterns. Most tend to occur in shades of orange, red or green, and specimens containing each of those colors are extremely nice when cut and polished.

To get to this vast location, take Highway 60 three miles east from where it intersects Interstate 10. At that point, which is at the western edge of Brenda, follow Perry Lane north from the highway three and one-half miles toward the mountains, bearing left at the fork, as shown on the map. From there, continuing at least another mile, agate and jasper can be found everywhere, on both sides of the road. In fact, the material is so plentiful that some portions of the landscape appear to be orange due to the large amount of colorful jasper lying on the ground.

Be advised that some of the material found here is porous, so be sure to allow sufficient time to find the best this location has to offer. Since there is so much available, most collectors do not bother hiking too far from the road. It is suggested you spend some time exploring regions a little farther away, since easily accessible spots seem not to have as much of the prized, solid, unpitted, multicolored material as do places more remote.

This entire area is situated in open desert, and there are many suitable places to set up a camp. Supplies are available in nearby Quartzsite.

Collecting at the Plomosa Mountain site

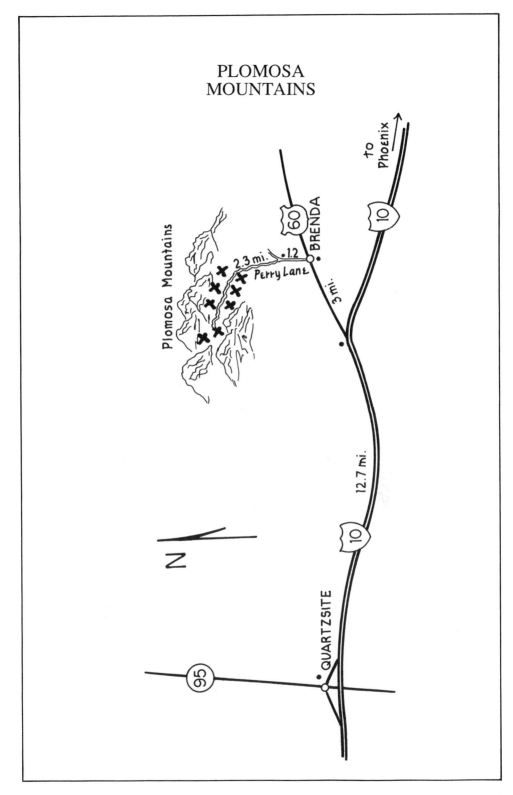

PLOMOSA
MOUNTAINS

53

JASPER
Brenda

The low volcanic hills known as the Bear Hills, a short distance east of Brenda, contain a large amount of very colorful jasper. Specimens show a variety of markings and inclusions including yellow and red flower patterns, moss, paisleys, and some unusual purple and blue streaks. In addition, there is a host of multicolored material, as well as some displaying only single shades of yellow, orange, purple or red. Pieces range from chips to sizeable chunks.

To get to this easily accessible collecting site, go east four and six-tenths miles on Highway 60 from where it intersects Interstate 10. This will be approximately one and one-half miles past Brenda and is the center of the collecting area. Be sure to pull well off the highway before stopping. There is a good place to do that about four-tenths of a mile further east, and it is suggested you proceed to that spot for safety reasons. Jasper is found throughout the hills on either side of the pavement, but primarily to the south. It is necessary to crawl under the highway fence to get to the mountain of jasper, but that isn't too difficult. Once past the fence, simply hike around the foothills and you should be able to pick up as much of the colorful cutting material as desired.

Approximately seven-tenths of a mile east of Brenda is a road leading north from the highway. That road goes to some old lead mines where collectors can find good mineral specimens on the dumps. Follow the somewhat dim and rough tracks about three miles to the mountains. This trek is only for four-wheel drive units.

Cabochons of moss jasper

JASPER
BRENDA

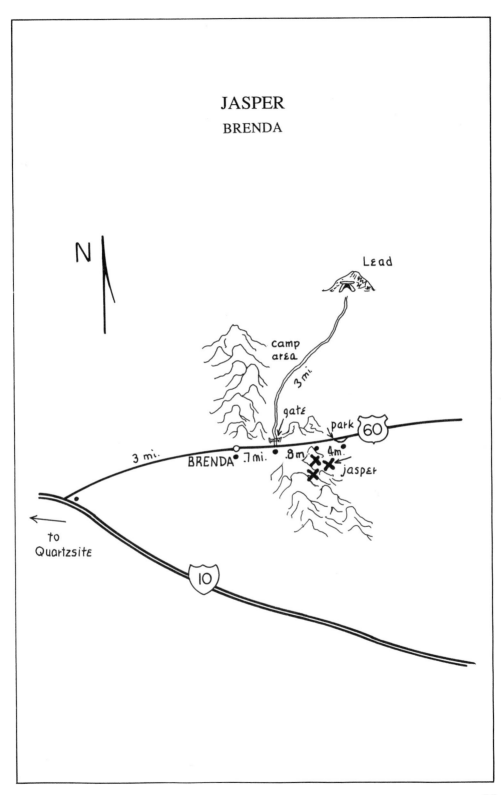

N

Lead

camp
area

3 mi.

gate

park

60

3 mi.

BRENDA • .7mi. • .8m. • 4m.

jasper

to
Quartzsite

10

CRYSTALS
Aguila

Nice quartz crystals, singles and clusters, can be obtained by following Eagle Eye Road north from Aguila as it climbs onto Indian Summit. The pavement ends after two miles and it gets very sandy at the three and nine-tenths miles point. Four-wheel drive will probably be necessary from time to time for the next two miles. After having gone six miles from the highway you will be at a gate. Be sure to close it after passing through, and continue along the road as it heads up the mountain. At the summit, there is a three way fork. Bear right, and go another nine-tenths of a mile. This section is rough, but most rugged vehicles should have no trouble. From there, proceed right again, and follow the tracks about two-thirds of a mile to the cliffs. Straight ahead is a dim trail going around the ridge to the crystal bearing quartz veins.

Some crystals can be found lying on the ground below the veins, but the best are extracted from pockets and cavities in the host rock. This, of course, requires some tough labor with gads, chisels and sledge hammers to expose and remove the crystal bearing regions. Size varies from micromount to over two inches in length and specimens range from perfectly clear to milky, with some exhibiting a faint pink hue. There are a number of adequate places to camp at the summit, including the site parking area. Some of these upper regions offer spectacular views of the desert down below.

Crystals from the Aguila site

CRYSTALS
AGUILA

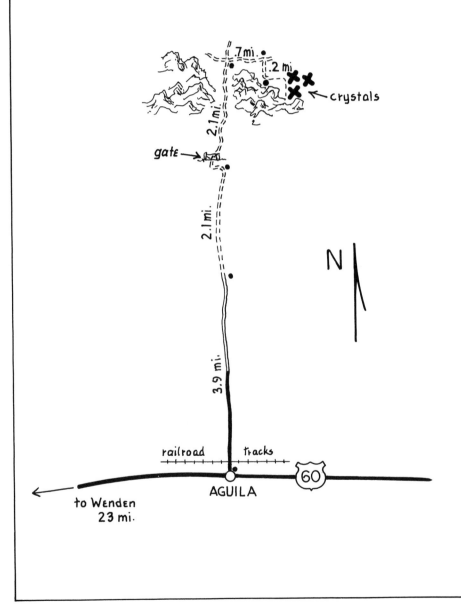

.7 mi.

.2 mi.

crystals

2.1 mi.

gate

2.1 mi.

N

3.9 mi.

railroad   tracks

60

AGUILA

to Wenden
23 mi.

MARBLE
Wenden

Marble, in shades of pink, yellow and orange, with vivid contrasting bands and inclusions running throughout, can be obtained in the mountains southeast of Wenden. This material is solid enough to take a good polish and can be used to produce exquisite cabochons, spheres and bookends. Some of the marble contains crystal filled cavities and such pieces, if encased in colorful marble, make beautiful display pieces, whether polished or left in their natural state.

To get to this very productive, but somewhat remote location, start one and eight-tenths miles east of Wenden on the dirt road heading south away from the black U.S. Manganese stockpile. Go through the gate, be sure to reclose it, and proceed along the pipeline road seven and three-tenths miles. At that point, turn left, doubling back toward the mountains one and one-tenth miles. From there the going gets rough. The roughness is caused by large chunks of marble all over the road and it might prove fruitful to stop and examine some of it. To get to the center of the collecting area, however, proceed one more mile to where the ridge meets the road.

Marble is scattered all over the surrounding terrain, having come from large seams in the mountain. Simply start exploring the area, trying to spot material with the best color and banding. Some pieces must be split, due to surface weathering, in order to properly discern the hidden interior quality.

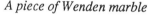

A piece of Wenden marble

MARBLE
WENDEN

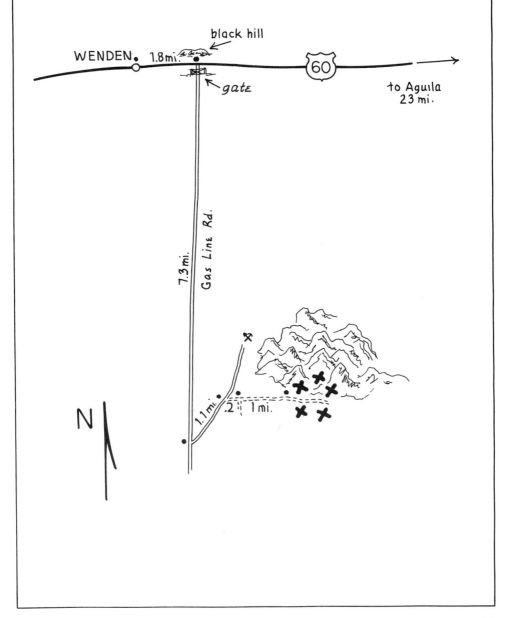

black hill

WENDEN • 1.8 mi.

60

to Aguila
23 mi.

gate

7.3 mi.

Gas Line Rd.

N

1.1 mi. .2 1 mi.

HEMATITE-JASPER
Bouse

This site features nice botryoidal hematite and colorful jasper and is fairly easy to get to. Much of the hematite will take a nice polish, but well formed botryoidal specimens are best left as is, for display in a mineral collection. The jasper occurs in shades of yellow, orange and red, and it also can be cut and polished nicely.

To get to the site from Bouse, go west on Plomosa Road, following the yellow center line, as it heads out of town. Proceed three and one-tenth miles to a cattle guard, and then, just three-tenths of a mile further, a road will be seen heading off to the right. Follow that road one and three-tenths miles to the start of the collecting area. From that point, continuing at least another mile west, you will be able to find the hematite and jasper scattered throughout the terrain for quite a distance. It isn't too difficult to find a good number of fine specimens by simply roaming the hillsides on either side of the road, but, as is usually the case, it seems the further from the road you go, within limits, the larger the pieces become. The hematite is black or brown and thereby not tough to spot against the lighter colored soil. The largest specimens of either mineral can be obtained by digging in the seams situated in the foothills. This involves hard work, but the potential rewards help make it more bearable. Just look for signs of where others have been digging.

Be advised that there are a few mining claims in the area, so be sure not to trespass onto any of them.

Collecting in one of the Bouse digging sites

HEMATITE AND JASPER

BOUSE

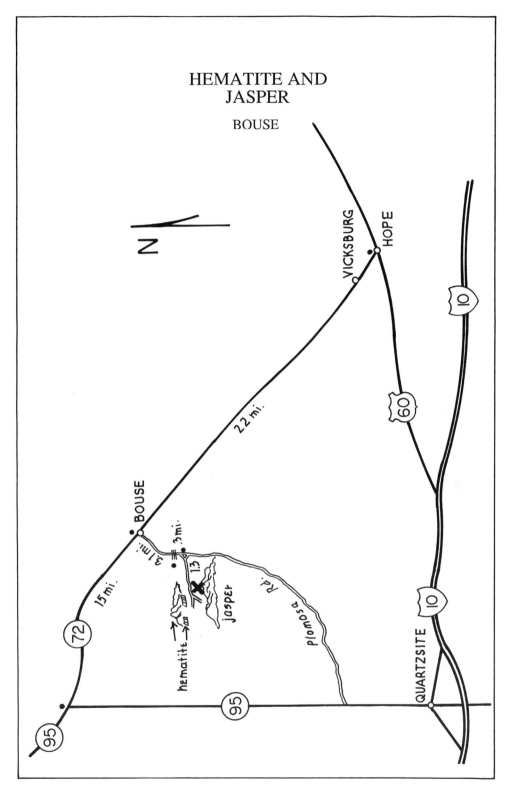

N

BOUSE

22 mi.

VICKSBURG

HOPE

10

U.S. 60

BOUSE

.3 mi.

.3 mi.

1.3

jasper

Plomosa Rd.

hematite

15 mi.

72

95

95

QUARTZSITE

10

WOOD
Moon Mountain

This remote site is not easy to get to and the trip should be attempted only in four-wheel drive. The location boasts fine petrified wood specimens and occasional chunks of colorful agate and jasper.

To get there from Quartzsite, go north from town one and eight-tenths miles either on Avenue 24E or Moon Mountain Road, and then jog to connect with the continuation of Moon Mountain Road, as shown on the map. Continue on this dirt road four and three-tenths miles to a fork. Stay to the right and continue an additional eighteen and two-tenths miles, bearing toward the distant cliffs in the northwest.

You will cross a number of washes along the way, but it is difficult to get off the main road. Just keep bearing to the northwest, following the sometimes dim tracks. At the proper mileage you will find yourself in yet another big wash, near the edge of some dirt hills. The wood is scattered throughout the hills, along with agate, jasper and jasp-agate.

It is recommended that you continue along the base of the hills another two and three-tenths miles to where the wash turns to the west. There, you can pull out of the sand and the hills are less steep.

Take some time to explore as much of this vast area as possible. The material close to the access road is not plentiful but an adequate amount can be picked up with a little patience.

One can find limb sections, in very large sizes, as well as delicate, perfectly formed twigs. The wood is primarily light brown and takes an excellent polish, often with orange streaks running throughout. The finest jasper is vivid red with white and blue stringers, being some of the most unusual I have ever found. It is scarce, but well worth looking for.

The dirt mounds at the collecting site

WOOD
MOON MOUNTAIN

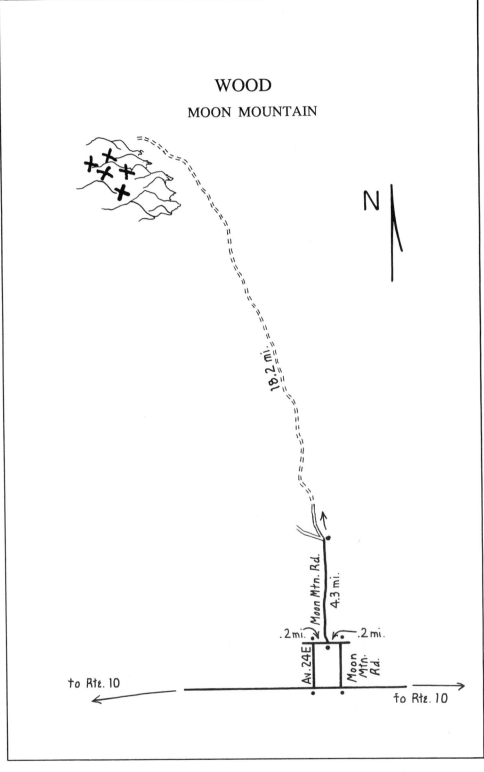

N

18.2 mi.

Moon Mtn. Rd.

4.3 mi.

.2 mi.   .2 mi.

Av. 24E   Moon Mtn. Rd.

to Rte. 10   to Rte. 10

MINERALS
Quartzite

These two sites provide collectors with a wide range of interesting minerals including onyx, quartz and ilmenite. To get there from Quartzsite, take the westernmost freeway overpass south to the frontage road and parallel the interstate three and nine-tenths miles to where you will spot some ruts heading into the hills. Follow those ruts six tenths of a mile to the crossroad and then turn west another one-half mile. At that point, go south and continue four-tenths of a mile to Site A where you can find chert, as well as nice, beautifully patterned brown onyx all over the hill. Both take a fairly good polish.

To get to Site B, return to the frontage road and go west another eight-tenths of a mile, then turn south one and seven-tenths miles behind the hills, as shown on the map. You will be able to see the mine dumps on the hills, a few hundred yards away, those being the primary sources for fine specimens of ilmenite and other minerals. The metallic ilmenite frequently displays black platelike crystallization, and stands out beautifully against the exceptionally white host quartz. Such pieces make very nice additions to a mineral collection.

Since the status of mines seems to change almost daily, BE CERTAIN, when you visit, that collecting is still allowed on those dumps. If you have any concerns about the status of the mines, restrict yourself to washes and terrain below.

The road to Site A

MINERALS
QUARTZSITE

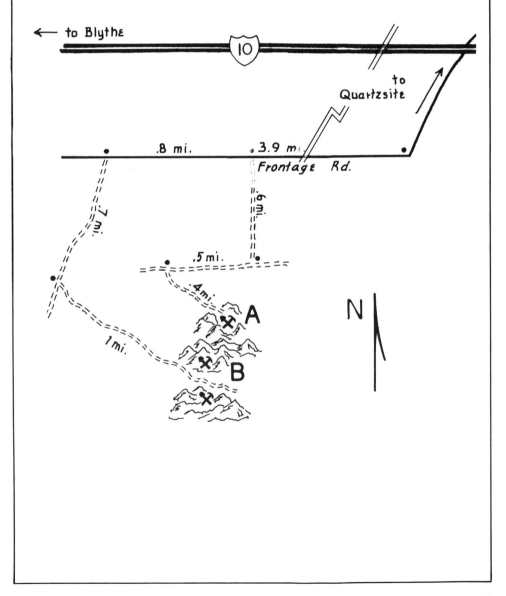

← to Blythe

10

to Quartzsite

.8 mi.

3.9 m.

Frontage Rd.

.7 mi.

.6 mi.

.5 mi.

.4 mi.

A

1 mi.

B

N

CRYSTAL HILL

This location is undoubtedly one of Arizona's best known rockhounding sites and, as the name implies, furnishes collectors with lots of nice quartz crystals. To get there, take Highway 95 south from Quartzsite nine miles to the B.L.M. sign designating the turn to Crystal Hill. The road heads east for six miles, is well maintained, and can be traversed by most vehicles. At the campground there are restrooms and cleared campsites. There is no water, however, so if you plan to spend some time, be sure to bring some.

The actual collecting is done in the wash to the north of the campground and on the hills opposite the wash. You can see the quartz seams from below, since the cliffs are loaded with diggings that form a near perfect line.

There are two types of rockhounds who collect at Crystal Hill. One is the ambitious hard-rock collector who chips into the tough host rock, attempting to split the seams and free the beautiful crystals from their placer on the mountain. This method involves hard work but the rewards are great if you discover a pocket. The other more popular means of collecting is to sift through the soil on top of the hill, beneath the dumps, and in the wash below, with a screen looking for loose crystals.

Some of the crystals have natural inclusions, many of which never have been identified. Double terminated crystals are also common and a few scepter crystals have been found here.

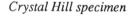

Crystal Hill specimen

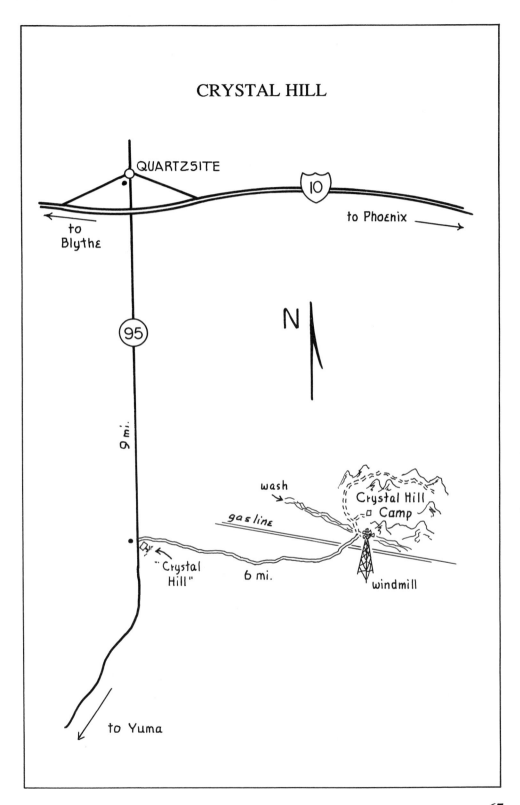

CRYSTAL HILL

QUARTZSITE

10

to Phoenix

to Blythe

95

N

9 mi.

wash

gasline

Crystal Hill Camp

"Crystal Hill"

6 mi.

windmill

to Yuma

CHALCEDONY ROSES
Porter Bed

This is a somewhat remote collecting site, but offers rockhounds an opportunity to gather nice chalcedony roses, some of which are quite sizeable. If you choose to make the journey, a rugged vehicle is necessary and it is a good idea to take some extra supplies in the event you are delayed.

To get there, proceed south from Quartzsite nine miles on Highway 95 to the Crystal Hill turnoff. Follow that road six miles to Crystal Hill and then jog to the pipeline road, as shown on the map, continuing another twelve miles. At the given mileage, park and explore the surrounding terrain.

Some of the best roses are found still encased within the tough host rhyolite where they were formed. The best of those primary sources can be seen from where you park. Look south across the wash to the second escarpment on the ridge, that being a most prolific spot. If you do trek to the ridge, it will be necessary to spend some time carefully examining it for roses that have been weathered out far enough so they can be removed without being damaged.

Numerous roses can also be found scattered throughout the flatlands. As shown on the map, this is an extensive area, so be sure to allow enough time for adequate exploration.

Some roses found here are colossal, often measuring many inches across. Another desirable attribute is that they all seem to fluoresce a bright greenish yellow, being welcome specimens for any collector with a fluorescent display.

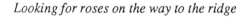

Looking for roses on the way to the ridge

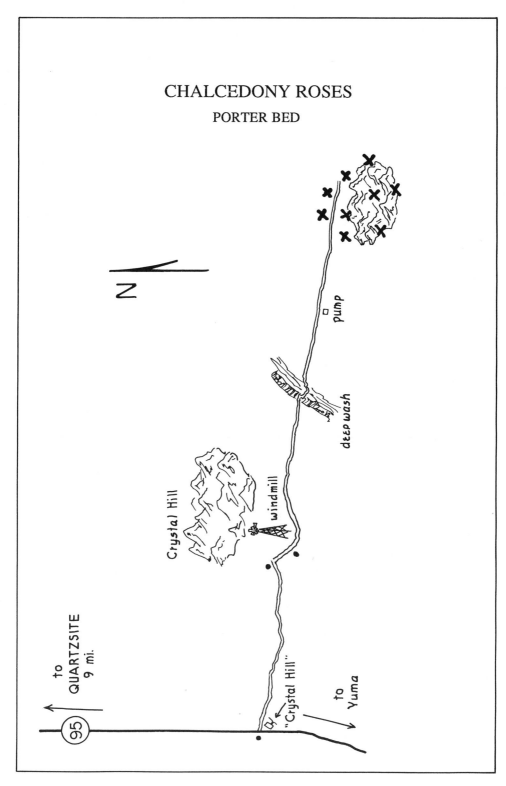

CHALCEDONY ROSES

PORTER BED

N

to
QUARTZSITE
9 mi.

95

Crystal Hill

windmill

deep wash

pump

"Crystal Hill"

to
Yuma

69

EAGLE TAIL MOUNTAINS

Copper minerals and fire agate can be found in the desert mountains about thirty four miles east of Quartzsite. To get there from Interstate 10, take the Hovater Road Exit (Exit 53) and go south three-tenths of a mile, across the aqueduct, to the frontage road. From there, turn right, travel one-tenth of a mile and then turn left onto Harquahala Road, proceeding another eight-tenths of a mile. Just as the road starts to curve, ruts will be seen leading south to some mine dumps in the hills. Go as far as your vehicle can take you along those ruts and then hike the remaining distance to the old prospects.

A number of minerals can be found in the dumps including chrysocolla, malachite, pyrite, and bornite. The best specimens are obtained by doing some hard rock digging in the quartz seams, which involves difficult sledge hammer and chisel work. Occasionally, however, very good pieces can be procured by just digging through the dumps. Take plenty of water if you plan to hike to the holes. Watch for snakes.

The second site is on the opposite side of Interstate 10. To get there simply cross over the interstate, go north about six-tenths of a mile and park. The region on and surrounding the little hill to the west contains lots of agate, some of which shows fire. This is said to be a private claim held by the Quartzsite Gem and Mineral Society, and it may be necessary to pay the $3.00 annual membership dues in order to collect. Further information can be obtained in Quartzsite.

MINERALS
EAGLE TAIL MOUNTAINS

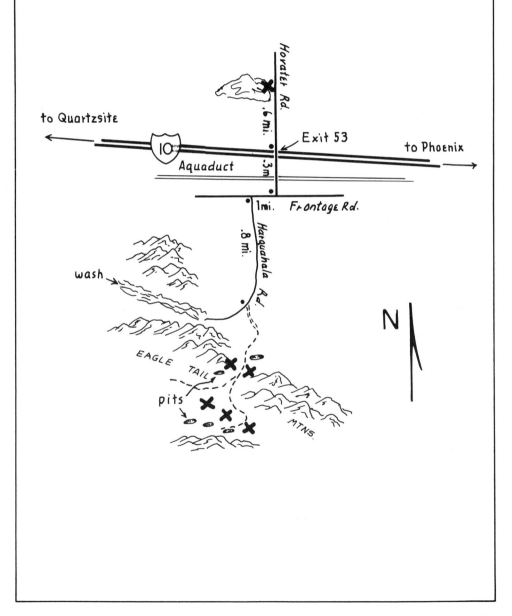

FIRE AGATES
KOFA

The location shown on the map is situated in the KOFA National Wildlife Refuge, a shelter for bighorn sheep and other animals. No digging or use of hand tools is permitted within the refuge, so minerals can only be picked up loose from the surface. That does limit the quantity of what can be obtained here, but it seems that new material is washed from the hills just about every time it rains. Be advised, however, that the fire agate is not overly plentiful, and it takes lots of patience and time to obtain a worthwhile quantity of those beautiful gemstones.

To get to this scenic location, go south on Highway 95 from Quartzsite about twenty seven and one-half miles to the ruins of Stone Cabin, as shown on the map. At that point, a road leads toward the mountains in the east, and that road should be followed another six and one-half miles to a fork. At the fork, bear right seven more miles and then turn west to the base of the mountains and start collecting.

Because this location is in the desert it is recommended only for the winter months and it is also essential that your vehicle be in good repair since it is somewhat remote.

Very fine chalcedony roses can be found throughout the desert flatlands starting from where you leave Highway 95 and continuing into the foothills. A few of the roses contain nice quartz crystals and make outstanding display pieces for a mineral collection.

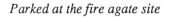

Parked at the fire agate site

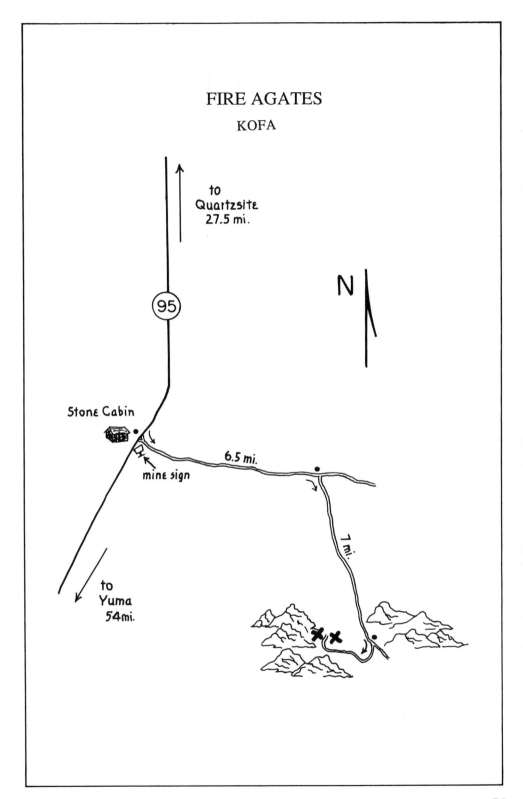

FIRE AGATES
KOFA

to
Quartzsite
27.5 mi.

N

95

Stone Cabin

6.5 mi.

mine sign

7 mi.

to
Yuma
54mi.

73

PASTELITE AND ORBICULAR JASPER

These three collecting areas provide a good variety of interesting materials and are relatively easy to get to. Site A is reached by going south from Quartzsite about nineteen miles on Highway 95 to the Palm Canyon turnoff and then following that well graded dirt road about two miles. From there, and continuing at least another three miles toward the mountains, rockhounds can find agate and chalcedony scattered throughout the terrain. This site is within the boundaries of the KOFA Wildlife Refuge, so rockhounds can only collect from the surface. No digging is allowed.

Continuing south on Highway 95 another six and one-tenth miles, a road will be spotted leading east from the pavement toward some hills. Go about one and one-half miles along that road to Site B, at the base of the mountains, and you will see where holes and trenches have been dug. The material found here is pastelite, and it looks like a good grade of jasper. Colors range from tan and pink to brown and red with some specimens quite sizeable.

Site C is reached by again returning to Highway 95 and going south another five and three-tenths miles. Here, you must carefully pull off the pavement and explore the wash and surrounding regions east of the road for interesting orbicular jasper. This brown material is filled with fascinating round spots or eyes, and can be used to make cabochons, spheres and book ends. The unusual jasper is found scattered throughout the area or dug from seams on the side of the small hills.

A specimen of orbicular jasper from Site C

PASTELITE AND
ORBICULAR JASPER

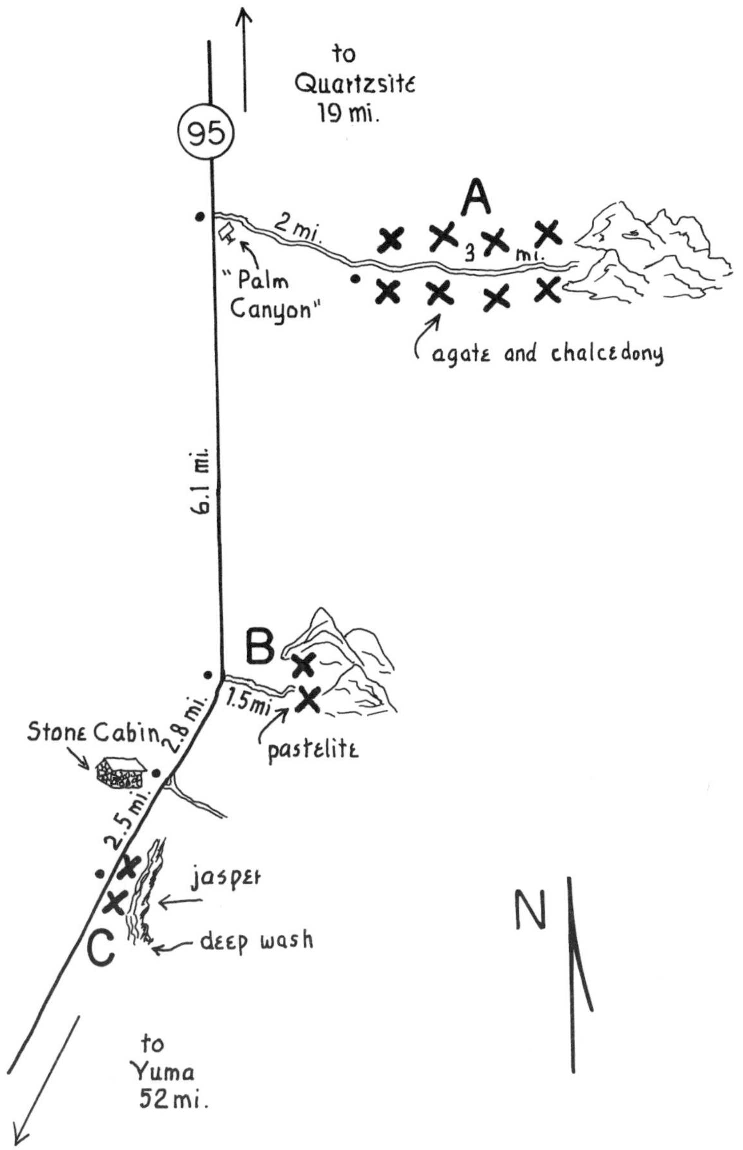

to
Quartzsite
19 mi.

A

2 mi.

"Palm
Canyon"

3 mi.

agate and chalcedony

6.1 mi.

B

Stone Cabin

2.8 mi.

1.5 mi.

pastelite

2.5 mi.

jasper

deep wash

C

N

to
Yuma
52 mi.

95

MINERALS
Castle Dome Area

This site boasts a number of fine minerals as well as petrified wood and banded rhyolite. To get there, take Highway 95 approximately thirty five miles north from Yuma to milepost 55. At that point, there is a road leading through the Yuma Proving Grounds to the KOFA Mountains. Follow that road about eight miles, abiding by all restrictions posted at the entrance. From that point, and extending at least another three miles, the terrain is littered with mine dumps. It is on those dumps where fine specimens of fluorite, vanadinite, calcite, anglesite and cerussite can be found. Be certain, however, that any mine you choose to explore is abandoned. At time of publication, a number of the once deserted dumps were again active. Do not trespass onto any active mining claim and be certain to stay out of all shafts.

In addition to the mines, the flatlands throughout this region are littered with often colorful rhyolite and occasional chunks of brown petrified wood. Be sure to take some time to search for those minerals, since they can be used to produce very nice polished pieces. Some material is covered with a dark desert varnish, and splitting may be necessary to properly discern what might be hidden beneath that exterior. Collecting in the KOFA Wildlife Preserve is restricted to surface gathering only. Do not do any digging.

This is regarded as one of the most scenic portions of the rugged KOFA Mountains and that helps to make it a most pleasant desert locality for a winter journey.

A view of the scenic collecting area

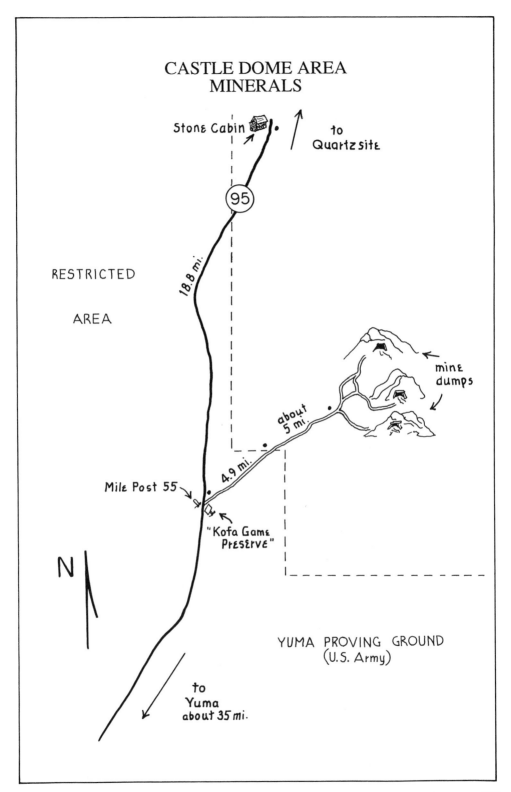

CASTLE DOME AREA
MINERALS

Stone Cabin

to
Quartzsite

95

RESTRICTED

AREA

18.8 mi.

mine
dumps

about
5 mi.

4.9 mi.

Mile Post 55

N

"Kofa Game
Preserve"

YUMA PROVING GROUND
(U.S. Army)

to
Yuma
about 35 mi.

GEODES, APACHE TEARS, GOLD
Aguila Area

Apache tears can be found strewn throughout the desert flatlands southeast of Aguila. To get there, simply go south out of town five miles and then bear left at the fork another seven miles. The site is reached just after passing through a big wash and the tears can be found scattered all over the terrain, on both sides of the road for quite a distance.

The exterior surface of the Aguila Apache tears is sometimes deceiving, being somewhat dull and opaque. Don't let that fool you, though, after polishing, most will indeed be transparent, with many displaying interesting bands or a silken sheen which produces spectacular cat's-eyes when polished. In addition to the tears, collectors can gather brilliant white chalcedony throughout the same area. Some of the chalcedony is banded and can be used to produce great cabochons.

Three and seven-tenths miles further along places you next to a small quarry just north of the road. In and around that old mine rockhounds can find chalcedony and little crystal filled, geode-like bubbles of limestone. These fascinating little orbs frequently make great display pieces in a mineral collection.

Be sure, while in the area, to continue to the old Vulture gold mine. This incredibly rich prospect was discovered in 1863 and proved to be one of Arizona's most productive mines. It is now inactive and being run as a museum. The small admission fee is well worth it.

Polished Aguila apache tears

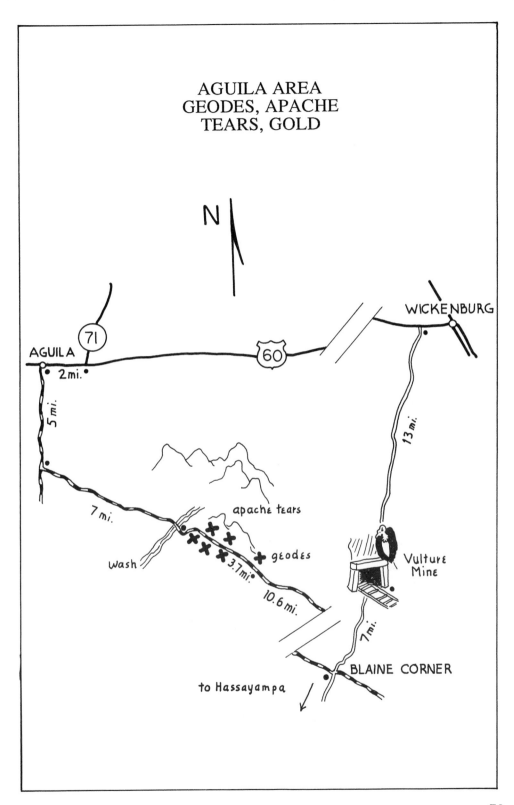

AGUILA AREA
GEODES, APACHE
TEARS, GOLD

N

WICKENBURG

AGUILA
71
2 mi.
60

5 mi.

13 mi.

7 mi.

apache tears

geodes

Wash

3.7 mi.

10.6 mi.

Vulture Mine

7 mi.

BLAINE CORNER

to Hassayampa

AGATE AND JASPER
Cave Creek

The region north of Carefree offers rockhounds a variety of collecting opportunities, as shown on the map. To get to the first, go east from Carefree toward Horseshoe Lake and, after having gone seven miles, bear left at the fork and continue another seven and six-tenths miles to Red Rover Mine Road. Proceed about one-half mile toward the mine and the ground is littered with some of the most vivid red jasper imaginable. This is Site A.

Site B is just one and eight-tenths miles past the Cave Creek Campground and also features the brilliant red jasper. Some of these chunks, however, are filled with intricate patterns, including delicate white lace motifs or black and white stringers.

Site C is another two and four-tenths miles further north and is the site of an old onyx mine. If the mine is not operating, some colorful cutting material can be gathered. Do not trespass if it appears the claim is again active.

Site D is one and nine-tenths miles further, and reached by turning left and rounding the little hill to where the road is washed out. From there, one can gather intricately patterned jasper and rhyolite.

Site E features beautiful agate strewn' throughout the hills, but the finest agate is obtainable across the road at Site F, this being the remnants of the Arizona Agate Mine. The mine has not been active for decades, but, if that is no longer the case, do not trespass. To reach the diggings, cross the stream and follow any of the numerous trails leading to the seams on the side of the cliff. Lots of the spectacular agate can be found on the hillsides, but the best is procured by using a chisel, gad and sledge hammer to remove it from its place in the mountain. This is some of the most colorful agate available anywhere in Arizona.

Inspecting an agate seam at Site F

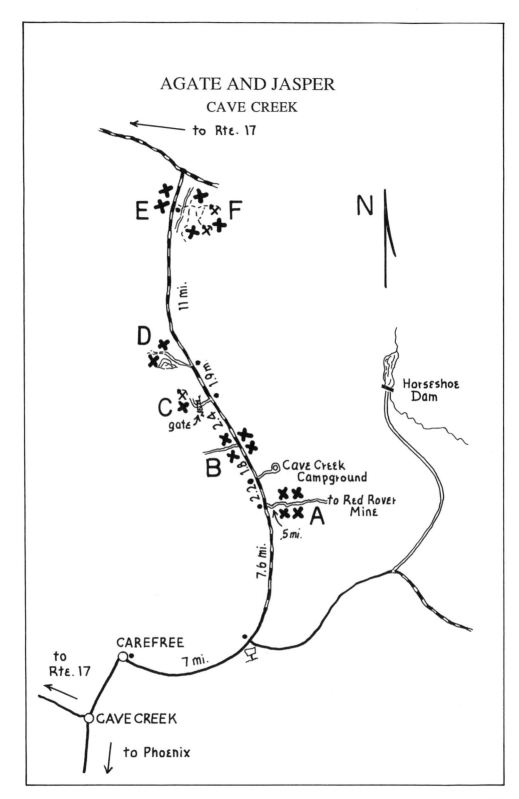

AGATE AND JASPER
CAVE CREEK

to Rte. 17

E F

N

11 mi.

D

1.9 mi.

C

gate

2.4 mi.

B

2.2 mi.

Cave Creek Campground

to Red Rover Mine

A

.5 mi.

7.6 mi.

Horseshoe Dam

CAREFREE

7 mi.

to Rte. 17

CAVE CREEK

to Phoenix

BLACK AGATE
Horseshoe Lake

Site A provides an opportunity for mineral collectors to gather fluorite, quartz and feldspar crystals. Most of the crystals are small, but if a number of them are concentrated within a single specimen, the resulting piece can frequently be used for display in a mineral collection. To get to Site A, take the road to Bartlett Lake out of Carefree and, after going seven miles, bear right at the fork. From that point, go another two and two-tenths miles. Be on the lookout for the turn as you approach the mileage, since it is difficult to spot and doubling back on this winding stretch of road is very difficult. Follow the ruts a short distance to the mine and search the dumps and surrounding territory for the minerals.

To get to Site B from Site A, return to the pavement, continue four more miles, and bear left another nine miles toward Horseshoe Lake. Just before reaching the caretaker's house, there is a field, on the left, and it is in that field where rockhounds gather the renowned Horseshoe Lake black agate.

Hike toward the light colored hills and you will be able to find agate in a variety of colors and patterns. Some is white or light blue, while other is a shimmering translucent black. A few of the latter pieces contain brilliant red regions, those being the most prized from this locality. In addition to the agate, one can pick up green and white, red and orange, and solid red jasper, all of which can be used to make beautiful polished pieces.

Parked at site B

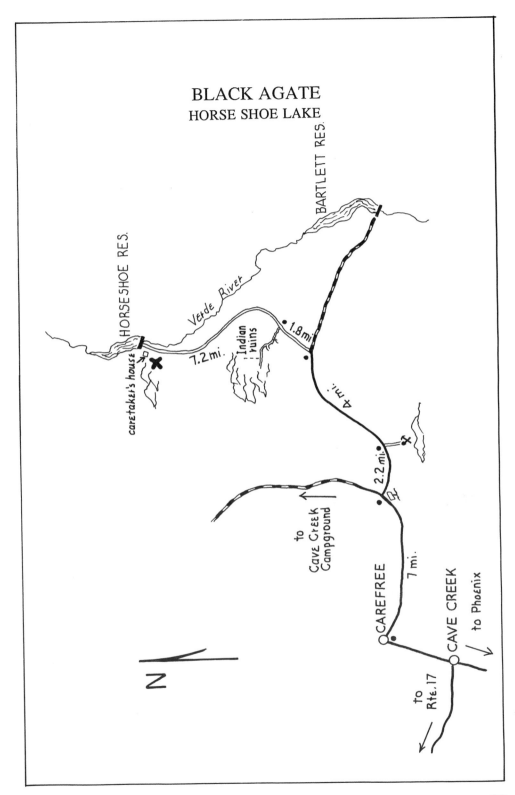

BLACK AGATE
HORSE SHOE LAKE

HORSESHOE RES.

BARTLETT RES.

Verde River

caretaker's house

Indian ruins

7.2 mi.

1.8 mi.

.4 mi.

2.2 mi.

to
Cave Creek
Campground

7 mi.

CAREFREE

CAVE CREEK

to Phoenix

to
Rte.17

N

RED JASPER
New River

There are three excellent sources of clean, bright red jasper along the road connecting Cave Creek and New River. To get there from Cave Creek, proceed toward Interstate 17 about two and one-half miles to New River Road. From there, turn right and jog through the new construction, as shown on the map, one and three-tenths more miles.

Site A is just past the bridge spanning Cave Creek and there are some ruts paralleling the creek on the north. Follow those ruts about three-tenths of a mile, but, if you do not have four-wheel drive, be very careful, since the loose sand can present some problems. Search the surrounding area for the brilliantly colored jasper. Some is much better than other, so take time to select only the best.

Site B is only three-tenths of a mile further north. Turn right from New River Road and follow the ruts about one-tenth of a mile. Red jasper is again scattered all over.

Site C, the final spot, is located one and two-tenths miles further north. At that point, turn right and follow the rough and steep tracks one and two-tenths miles, bearing right at the fork. This is the most productive of the three locations, but, as might be expected, also the toughest to get to. At the given mileage is a good flat spot to park and turn around. The red jasper, some of which is nearly purple, can be found all along the ruts as well as scattered throughout the lowlands.

RED JASPER
NEW RIVER

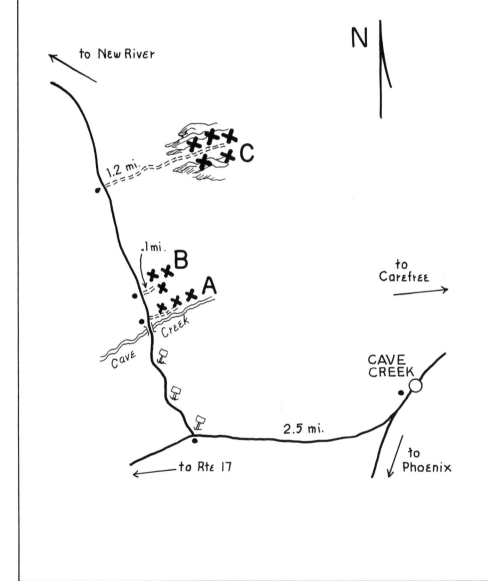

N

to New River

1.2 mi.

X X X
X C

.1 mi.
B
X X
X
X X X A

Cave Creek

to Carefree

CAVE
CREEK

2.5 mi.

to
Phoenix

to Rte 17

AGATE
Painted Rock - Rowley Mine Specimens

To get to the agate location, take Interstate 8 approximately five miles west of Gila Bend to the Painted Rock turnoff and head north about ten and one-half miles. The mountains will be on your right and some dim tracks will be spotted leading off to the northeast. Follow those tracks a short distance and you should be able to spot pieces of agate and small quartz crystals on the ground. From there, hunt toward the mountains. If you do not feel your vehicle is capable of traveling on the old road, simply park well off the pavement and hike to the collecting area. The agate is not extremely plentiful, but the colors and internal inclusions make the search worthwhile.

The old Rowley lead mine is located approximately one and one-half more miles toward Painted Rock Dam and is the source of some of the finest wulfenite specimens in the world. Not only is this a good place to find wulfenite, but the field tripper can also collect specimens of mimetite, cerussite and chrysocolla. This is considered a very dangerous mine, so be cautious, observe all warning signs and DO NOT ENTER ANY SHAFTS OR TUNNELS.

If you have time, be sure to visit Painted Rock State Park. There, you can see a small rocky mountain covered with ancient graffiti. It is fun to try to figure out what the symbols might mean and why they were etched there in the first place.

Painted Rock State Park

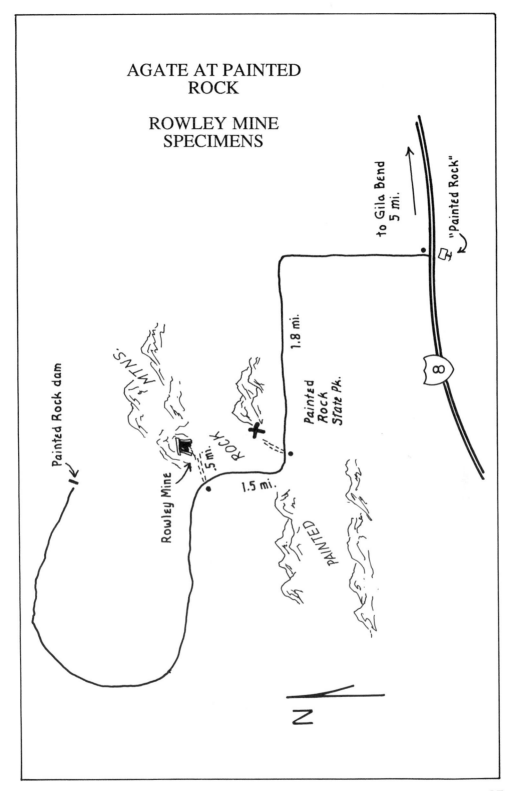

AGATE AT PAINTED ROCK

ROWLEY MINE SPECIMENS

to Gila Bend 5 mi.

"Painted Rock"

1.8 mi.

Painted Rock State Pk.

Painted Rock dam

ROCKY MTNS.

Rowley Mine

.5 mi.

1.5 mi.

PAINTED

8

N

Geodes from near Aguila

Wulfenite from Rowley Mine

Artifacts from Eastern Arizona

Agate specimens from Arizona

AGATE
Fourth Of July Peak

The beautiful banded agate found near Fourth of July Peak, north of Gila Bend, has made that area famous for years. To get there, take the Hassayampa Road north from town about thirty miles to Agua Caliente Road. The turnoff is well marked and opposite some large cattle pens, making it fairly easy to spot. From there, go west one and one-tenth miles and then bear right, off the pavement. Follow the well graded road fourteen and three-tenths miles and turn onto the tracks heading off to the right. Continue about six-tenths of a mile to the old chimney, that marking the center of Site A, the Chimney Beds. From there, in varying concentrations, all the way to Fourth of July Peak, agate can be found.

The agate is obtained by simply walking throughout the terrain and searching for telltale little white stones. Most of the agate has a white opaque exterior and can be found on the flatlands as well as in the wash or other areas of erosion. Interiors tend to be light grey, with very delicate, fine, concentric white bands. In addition to the banded material, one can also procure red, blue and grey moss agate, but it isn't plentiful and takes some patient searching to find. Most of what can be picked up from the surface is small, but by digging one can unearth larger specimens.

At Fourth of July Peak (Site B) rockhounds can obtain more of the banded agate, multicolored agate, crystals and even some Apache tears. As before, just roam through the surrounding countryside to find specimens.

Polished fire agates

90

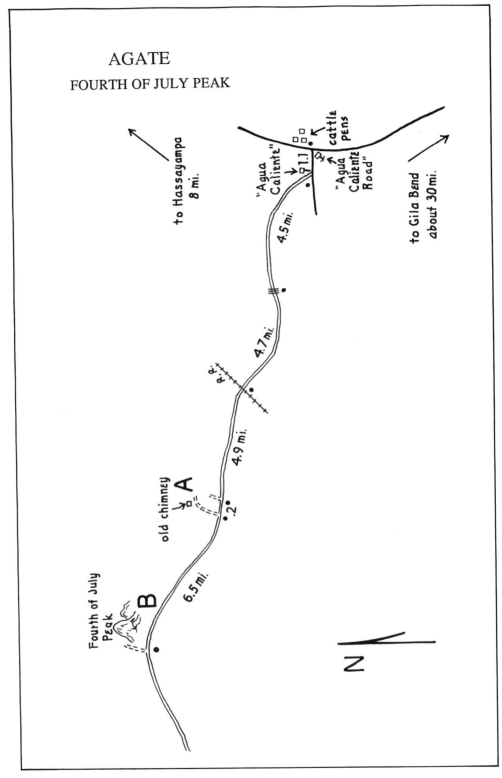

AGATE

FOURTH OF JULY PEAK

to Hassayampa
8 mi.

cattle pens

"Agua Caliente"

1.1

"Agua Caliente Road"

to Gila Bend
about 30 mi.

4.5 mi.

4.7 mi.

R.R.

4.9 mi.

old chimney

A

.2

Fourth of July Peak

B

6.5 mi.

N

FIRE AGATE
Saddle Butte

Saddle Mountain has been a premier southwest rock collecting spot for many years. Primarily, it is famous for the beautiful fire agate and chalcedony that litters the surrounding flatlands. In addition, rockhounds can occasionally find crystal filled geodes on the lower slopes.

To get to this fascinating spot, take the Tonopah exit from Interstate 10, which is about seventy five miles east of Quartzsite, and head south two and seven-tenths miles. Turn right onto the Salome Highway, continue five and one-tenth miles, turn left, proceed six-tenths of a mile and there will be some ruts heading toward the mountains on the south. Take any of them about one-half mile to the foothills.

From wherever you park at the base of the mountain the ground will be littered with chalcedony all the way back to the pavement. Some of that chalcedony contains regions of precious fire, so it is essential you carefully inspect all brown pieces.

Most of the primary fire agate deposits were located high on Saddle Mountain and have been worked out. Only a few such seams remain, but they are situated on dangerous steep faces and thereby inaccessible. There are, however, numerous chalcedony seams running through the mountain and some of them exhibit potential for containing fire. If you feel like doing some hard rock work with gads, chisels and sledge hammers, you should try your luck at splitting such seams in hopes of exposing some otherwise hidden fire agate.

A view of the Saddle Mountain collecting area

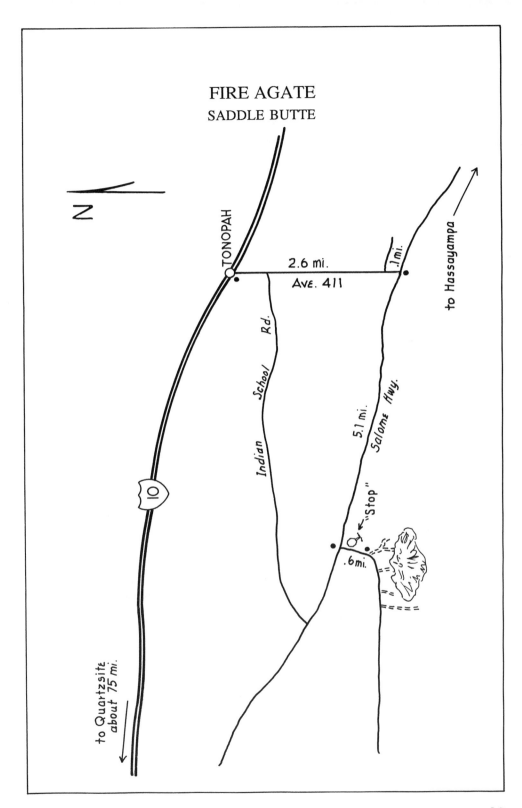

FIRE AGATE
SADDLE BUTTE

N

TONOPAH

2.6 mi.
Ave. 411

.1 mi.

to Hassayampa

Indian School Rd.

10

5.1 mi.

Salome Hwy.

"Stop"

.6 mi.

to Quartzsite
about 75 mi.

THE RED CLOUD MINE AREA

One of Arizona's most notable mining localities is situated along the eastern edge of the Colorado River, just north of Imperial Dam. This area is known as the Red Cloud District, and is made famous by the incredibly brilliant red-orange wulfenite specimens that have been found at the Red Cloud Mine.

Currently, the Red Cloud is closed to collectors, but that status changes from time to time. On the map, however, are listed a number of other mines in the region, all of whose dumps offer rockhounds a chance for finding mineral specimens. A partial list of what can be obtained includes calcite, barite, vanadinite and fluorite, some of which is well crystallized.

Listing of these mines DOES NOT imply permission to collect there, however. It will be necessary to visit any of interest and personally ascertain whether or not collecting is permitted. Under no circumstances should you enter any of the mine shafts, whether abandoned or not. The host rock in this area is very rotten and capable of collapsing as a result of even the slightest tap of a rock pick.

If you choose not to inspect any of the dumps, there is still a good chance for finding worthwhile specimens in the regions below them or in the Red Cloud Wash, the Black Rock Wash or the Yuma Wash, as shown on the map.

The road all the way to the Papago and Red Cloud mines is generally in good condition and most rugged vehicles should have no trouble getting that far. From the Red Cloud to the Clip, however, it is a different story. High clearance four-wheel drive is essential in order to make it.

It has been reported that many of the washes in this region also contain gold, so, if you have time and some dry washing equipment, it might be worth trying your luck.

To get to the mines you must cross the Yuma Proving Ground. Be certain to read all signs posted near Highway 95 and if a red flag is flying DO NOT ENTER! The flag indicates that live bombing is being conducted.

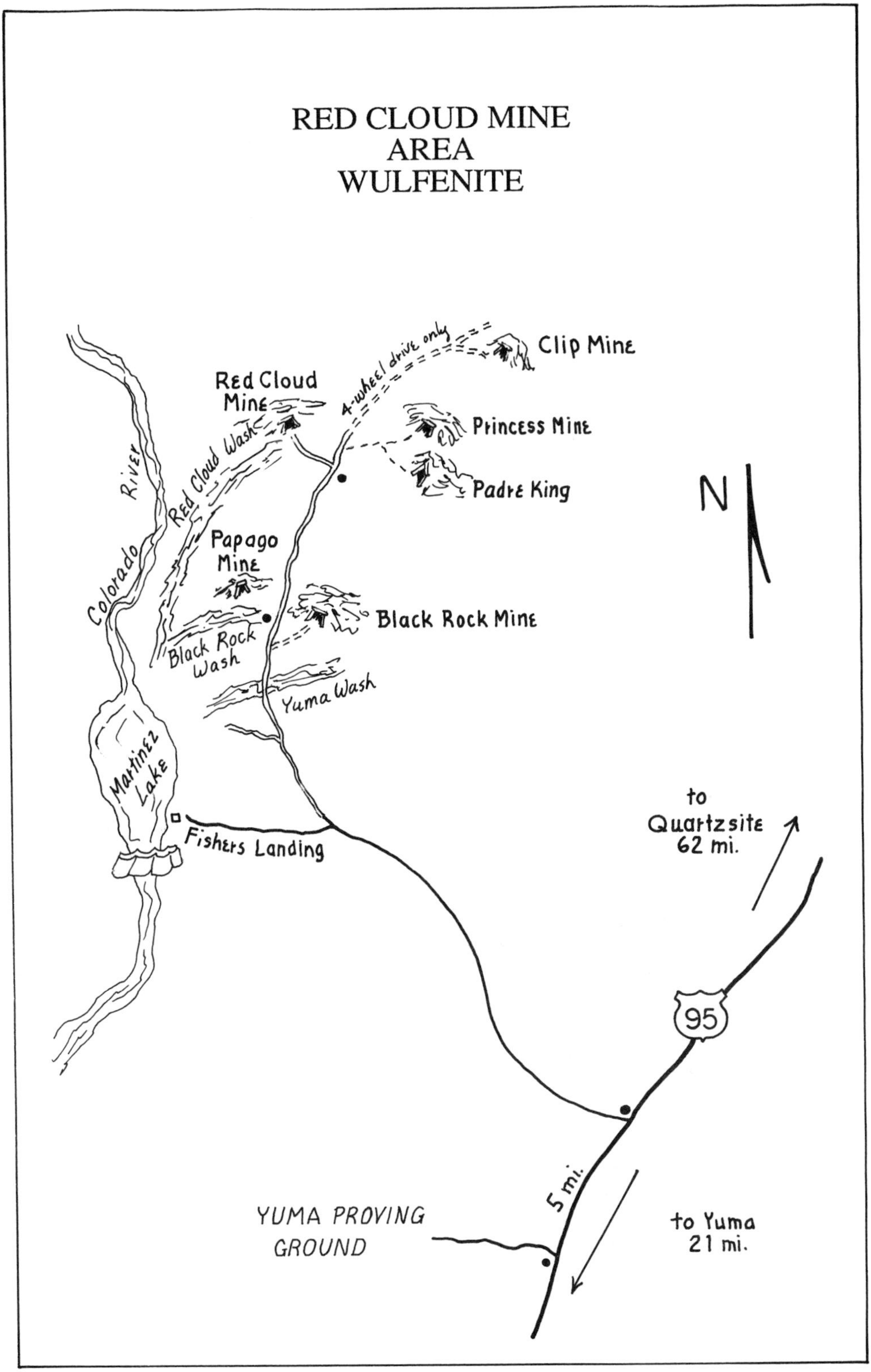

RED CLOUD MINE
AREA
WULFENITE

Clip Mine

Red Cloud Mine

4-wheel drive only

Princess Mine

Colorado River

Red Cloud Wash

Padre King

Papago Mine

N

Black Rock Mine

Black Rock Wash

Yuma Wash

Martinez Lake

to Quartzsite 62 mi.

Fishers Landing

95

YUMA PROVING GROUND

5 mi.

to Yuma 21 mi.

MARBLE
Queen Valley

Very nice, fine grained red and green marble can be collected in the shadows of the spectacular Superstition Mountains, not far from the town of Queen Valley. To get to this most productive location, go north on Queen Valley Road one and seven-tenths miles from where it intersects Highway 60. From there, turn right onto Hewitt Station Road, go three and three-tenths miles and then proceed north onto Forest Service Road 172. Some stretches of the Forest Service road are rough, so a rugged vehicle will be needed to make it all the way. Continue four and three-tenths miles and ruts will be encountered branching off to the right into a shallow canyon. Follow those ruts one-half mile or as far as your vehicle is capable of going. There is lots of loose sand here, so, unless you have four-wheel drive, it might be advisable to hike the rest of the way to the marble deposit rather than ride in your vehicle.

The site is easily spotted, being an old quarry and good samples of marble are scattered all over the terrain directly below the mine and strewn throughout the adjacent wash. Most collectors are satisfied with what can be procured from the rubble below the workings, but some like to tackle the seam itself with gads, bars and chisels. Granted, some beautiful material can be extracted using hard rock methods, but it is tough work. If you choose to attack the seam itself, be sure to wear gloves and goggles and have plenty to drink.

Seam at the collecting site   *On the dumps at the collecting site*

MARBLE
QUEEN VALLEY

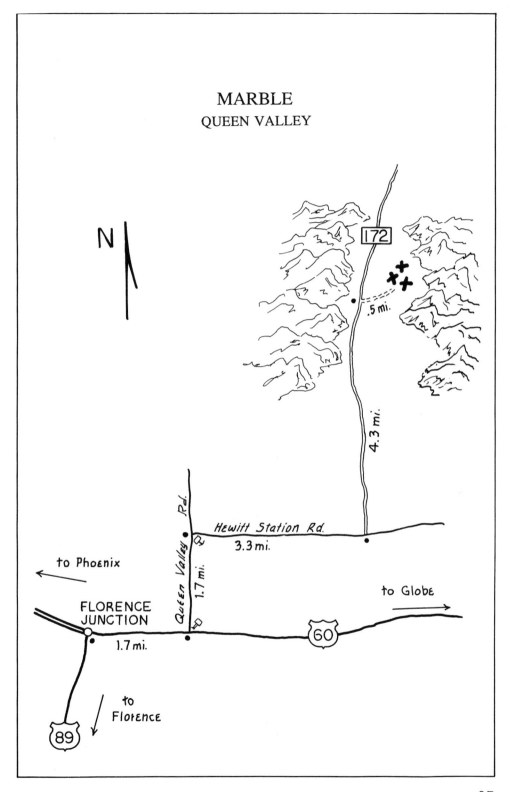

N

172

.5 mi.

4.3 mi.

Queen Valley Rd.

Hewitt Station Rd.
3.3 mi.

1.7 mi.

to Phoenix

FLORENCE
JUNCTION

to Globe

60

1.7 mi.

to
Florence

89

APACHE TEARS
Superior

Some of the finest Apache tears available anywhere come from a perlite deposit southwest of Superior. Most are gem quality and can be used for tumbling, cabbing or even faceting. This is a fee location, but the quantity and quality of what can be found more than compensates for the slight charge.

To get to this famous location, take Highway 60 west from Superior approximately one mile. There is a large sign on the south side of the highway denoting the Apache Tears Caves and it is there where you turn. Continue following the signs for about one and six-tenths miles to the buildings on top of the hill. The mine is open from 9:00 A.M. until 5:00 P.M. every day, and the fee, at time of publication, is $1.00 per bucket collected.

Visitors are not allowed to enter the old perlite mine, but the outer areas are graded and new material is turned up every day. Everywhere you look there are countless Apache tears, ranging in size from less than a quarter of an inch in diameter to some as large as an egg. It doesn't take much time to fill a bucket with the tears. Be sure to also take a few specimens that are still embedded in the host perlite. These make outstanding display pieces just the way they are.

The perlite, which is the predominant material here, is volcanic glass. Therefore, it is imperative to be cautious. Don't rub your eyes or face after handling it until you wash your hands.

At the collecting site

APACHE TEARS
SUPERIOR

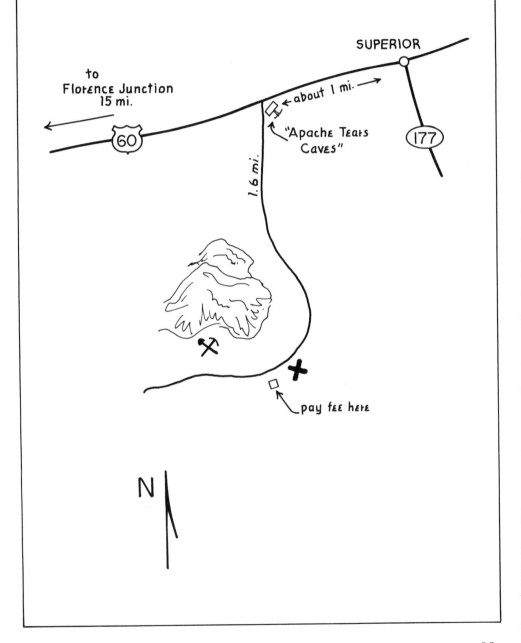

SUPERIOR

to
Florence Junction
15 mi.

← about 1 mi. →

60

177

"Apache Tears
Caves"

1.6 mi.

pay fee here

N

ONYX
Globe

    Some of the most colorful onyx available anywhere in Arizona comes from a deposit situated in the mountains northwest of Globe. To get there, take Highway 60 north from town 15.9 miles and, just as you pass the bridge over Seven Mile Wash, there will be a road heading to the west. From there, follow the instructions on the map to the collecting area. As you approach the proper mileage, look for the little turnout on the left. There isn't much room for more than a few cars, but it is the only adequate place to park off the road near the onyx deposit.

    From there you must hike. It isn't a bad trek, and taking the old washed out road to the easy-to-see onyx seam, is much easier than cross country hiking through the thorn bushes and brush. This road is not passable, however, by any but the most rugged four-wheel drive units, and I wouldn't recommend trying to drive it.

    Colors vary from near solid white, to pieces swirled and/or layered with red, pink, white, grey and yellow. Plenty of this top quality onyx can be found scattered all over the hillside below the seam itself and most collectors are satisfied with what can be gathered from that material. Incredibly beautiful pieces, however, can also be removed from their place in the mountain with gads, chisels and pry bars. This is tough work, but the rewards for the labor are often worth it. Be sure to wear goggles when directly working the seam.

A portion of the onyx seam

ONYX
GLOBE

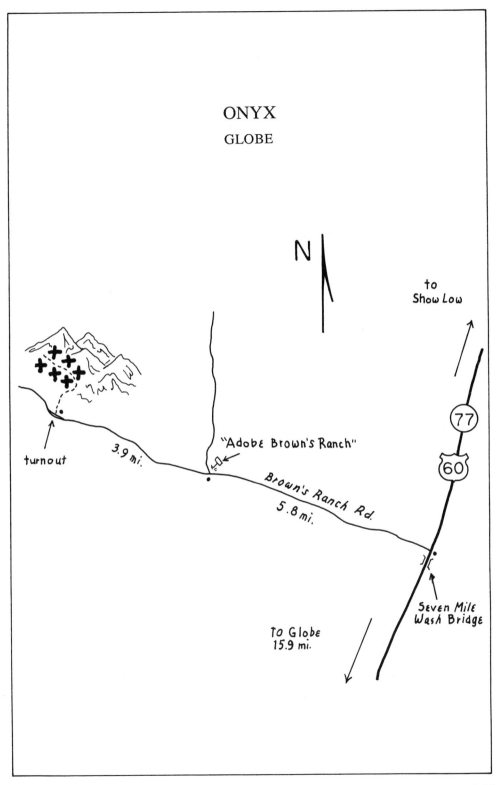

N

to
Show Low

turnout

3.9 mi.

"Adobe Brown's Ranch"

Brown's Ranch Rd.

5.8 mi.

77

60

Seven Mile
Wash Bridge

To Globe
15.9 mi.

FIRE AGATES
Safford Area

This easy to reach site is designated as the Black Hills Rockhound Area by the Bureau of Land Management and is open to everybody.

To reach the fire agate field, go 10 miles east of Safford to State Highway 666 and then proceed north ten and one-half miles to milepost 141. The turnoff is just three-tenths of a mile further, as shown on the map. Go through the cattle guard and follow the ranch road about one and one-half miles. It is a fairly good gravel road, but passenger cars may find it difficult in spots. Cross a small wash and then climb to the campground and collecting area.

Chalcedony can be found scattered all over the terrain stretching for quite a distance. The prime material to be collected here is, of course, the brownish chalcedony exhibiting colorful fire. It doesn't take long to find pieces with traces of brown and gold indicating the potential for fire, but most of what is picked up will not contain the highly desirable bursts of color. Be patient and willing to do some exploring, however, and you should be able to gather an acceptable quantity of the gemstones.

Best success is generally had by climbing the little mountain to the east of the registration sign or roaming the nearby hills. Chalcedony litters the ground, and some is still embedded in the mountain. In addition to either working the deposits in the mountain or picking up specimens from float, digging can also provide you with fine specimens.

Return to the highway and continue to Thumb Butte on the right, as illustrated on the map. In the area around the Butte and in washes to the south, collectors can find small agate nodules, pieces of petrified palm root and Apache tears.

Leaving the Black Hills rock hounding area

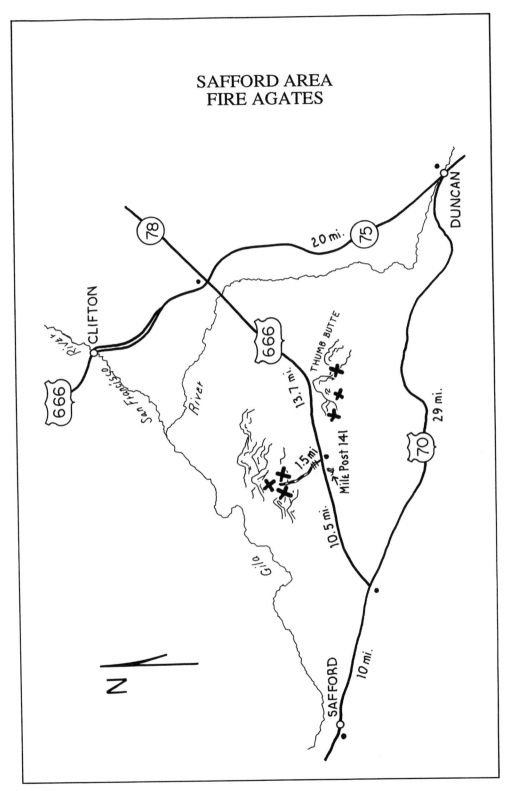

SAFFORD AREA
FIRE AGATES

AGATES
Clifton Area

The region surrounding prominent Mulligan Peak, just northeast of Clifton, boasts lots of nice and frequently large agate nodules and geodes. The agate is often intricately banded with beautiful fortification patterns and colors range from deep purple to lavender and gray. Chips and pieces are scattered all over the terrain, but the large nodules are primarily obtained by digging them from the ground like potatoes. They occur just under the top soil, and some are still in place within the host rhyolite where they formed.

This is not an easy area to reach (see map). To get there from Clifton, take the SECOND bridge crossing the San Francisco River, bear left and go about two miles to the entrance of Limestone Canyon. From there, four-wheel drive is probably necessary, since the ruts weave in and out of a sandy wash. The first trail leading to the digging area exits the Limestone Canyon road after about one-half mile and is on the right. It is tough to spot, so be sure to watch closely as you approach the given mileage.

The trail leads up the steep slopes to Mulligan Peak's southwest side and the trek is tough. At trail's end you should be able to see where others have dug before. Look for pieces of agate and other debris as indicators as to where you should start.

There is another collecting area on the opposite side of the mountain and it is reached by continuing along the Limestone Canyon road approximately one more mile. At that point you should see the remnants of an old cabin and a gate. Go through the gate and follow the road that branches to the right. You will encounter some water troughs and pipes and eventually a very large boulder on the side of the hill with a trail leading toward it. That marks the center of the agate field. As before, some material will be found on the surface, but the best is generally obtained by digging.

Be sure to carry plenty of water, since this is a long and arduous hike and the temperature can get very hot during the day.

Polished agates from the Clifton area

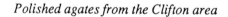

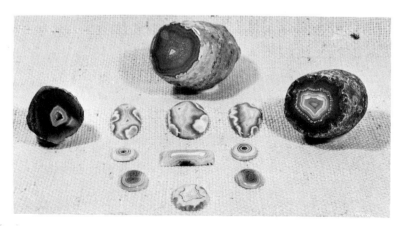

CLIFTON AREA
AGATES

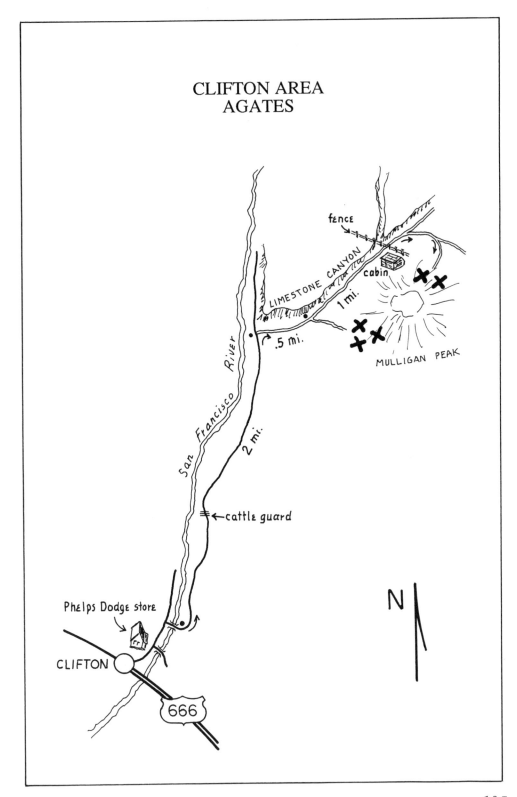

fence

LIMESTONE CANYON

cabin

1 mi.

MULLIGAN PEAK

San Francisco River

.5 mi.

2 mi.

cattle guard

Phelps Dodge store

rr

CLIFTON

666

N

FIRE AGATE
Clifton

These sites offer collectors very nice plume and flower agate, as well as chalcedony and precious fire agate. To get to the wash which marks the first location, take Highway 666 to the school situated at the southern edge of Clifton. From there, go under the bridge, proceed five miles to a fork, bear left and continue another six-tenths of a mile. Instead of heading into Loma Linda Estates, go right, down the hill, to where a wash crosses the road. It is in and around this wash where one can find the chalcedony, some of which is filled with fire.

Common chalcedony is fairly plentiful here, and much contains areas of brown, indicating the potential for fire. Color filled fire agate, however, is not abundant. It takes patience and determination to find the gem material, but it is well worth the effort. Carry a canteen of water or a moist rag to wet suspicious stones. The wetting helps to bring out fire if there is any.

As you walk through the wash, don't hesitate to rake through the soft sand or move some boulders. It is in places like those that prize specimens can be hidden.

From the wash, follow the road up the hill for about one and four-tenths miles to a gate. Search there for desert roses and agate. Another two and eight-tenths miles places you next to a little hill. The terrain surrounding that hill is randomly littered with chalcedony, agate and crystals. The agate comes in a variety of colors with numerous interesting inclusions, including some exhibiting exquisite plume and/or flower patterns. Most are small and nothing here is overly plentiful.

Rough fire agates from Clifton

106

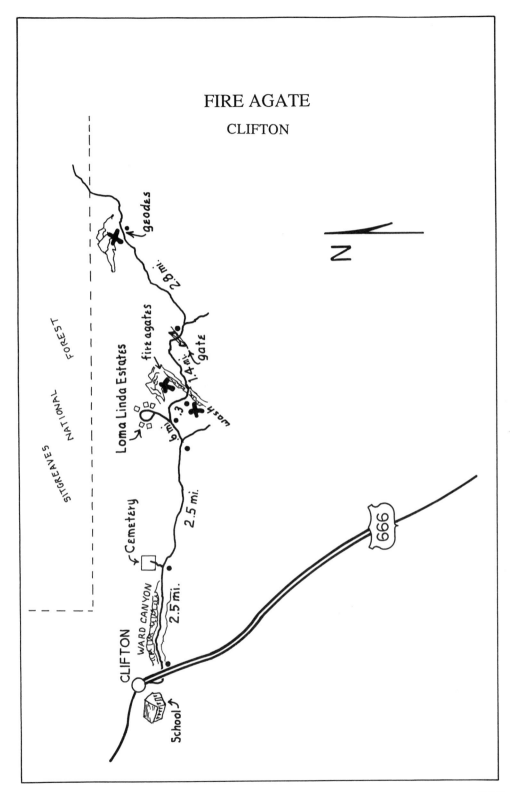

FIRE AGATE
CLIFTON

N

geodes

2.8 mi.

fire agates

1.4 mi.

gate

SITGREAVES   NATIONAL   FOREST

Loma Linda Estates

wash

.3 mi.

.9 mi.

Cemetery

2.5 mi.

666

CLIFTON

WARD CANYON

2.5 mi.

School

107

CARLYLE MINE DUMPS

The dumps of the old Carlyle Mine provide rockhounds with amethyst, pyrite cubes, and a host of other minerals. It is a rough journey to the collecting site, and the trip should only be attempted in rugged vehicles. To get there, take Highway 75 north from Duncan one and one-tenth miles to Carlyle Road and turn east off the pavement. Proceed another thirteen and one-half miles into the mountains to where a mine dump will be encountered on the left. Also at that point is a sign designating this now to be Summit Peak Road and tracks lead off to the right toward the central mining area.

At time of publication, there was some active mining being done in the region and, for safety reasons, permission was required before doing any collecting. To obtain that consent, proceed to the office, as shown on the map. If nobody is there, search only on unposted dumps along Summit Peak Road.

Remember that old dumps can be very dangerous, making it essential to always be on the lookout for abandoned pits covered with decaying timbers, broken glass and rusty nails.

Continuing along Summit Peak Road you will encounter numerous additional dumps, any one of which offers good collecting possibilities. At the three and one-half mile mark, lots of colorful jasper, chert and agate can be found scattered throughout the washes and flatlands.

The highway can be reached by continuing along this road thirteen more miles, bearing left at major forks.

An old dump at the jasper mine

CARLYLE MINE
DUMPS
MINERALS

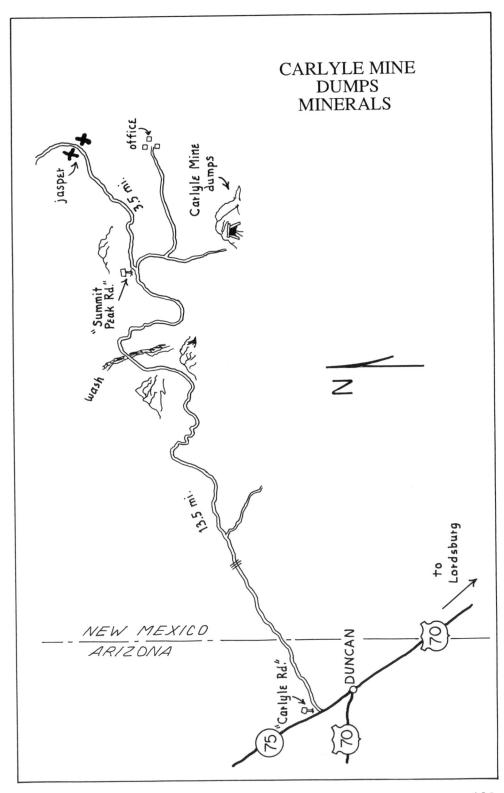

jasper

office

3.5 mi.

Carlyle Mine
dumps

"Summit Peak Rd."

wash

N

13.5 mi.

to
Lordsburg

NEW MEXICO
ARIZONA

DUNCAN

"Carlyle Rd."

75

70

70

FIRE AGATE
Round Mountain

This area features chalcedony roses and beautiful fire agate. To get there from Duncan, head south on Highway 70 approximately twelve miles to milepost five. From there, the turnoff is only six-tenths of a mile further. At the proper mileage, go left and proceed seven and one-tenth miles to where a B.L.M. sign instructs you to turn left again. Rugged vehicles are recommended, since the road is not regularly maintained and is rough in places. Be sure to also bring plenty of water and gas, since this is a most remote area.

After having gone about 2.5 miles, desert roses and fire agates can be found all along the road, and it might be worth your time to stop and do a little searching. The start of the primary site, however, is another two and one-half miles further and, at that point, a cattle guard and gate will be encountered. Go through the gate and follow the loop road around the mountain to what is generally regarded as being the most productive of the Round Mountain collecting areas. This is probably because few people get that far due to the roughness of the road.

Roam throughout the flatlands, paying particularly close attention to any brown or gold chalcedony. It won't take much time to locate such pieces, those having the most potential for exhibiting the beautiful and highly prized fire. Be patient and willing to spend sufficient time here and you should be rewarded with some spectacular gemstones.

FIRE AGATE
ROUND MT.

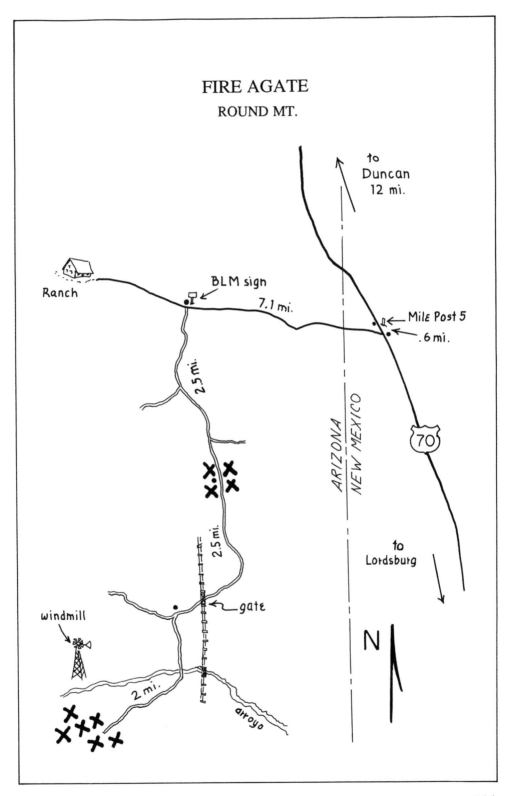

to Duncan 12 mi.

Ranch

BLM sign

7.1 mi.

Mile Post 5

.6 mi.

2.5 mi.

ARIZONA
NEW MEXICO

70

2.5 mi.

gate

to Lordsburg

windmill

2 mi.

arroyo

N

AGATE-GEODES

Lots of quality agate and chalcedony can be gathered at this somewhat remote location. To get there, go south from Duncan about nineteen miles to milepost 12. From there, continue seven-tenths of a mile further and turn right, proceeding on the main road thirteen and four-tenths miles to a corral. Drive through the gate, closing it after passing through, and follow the ruts paralleling the fence on the right. Another gate will be encountered about two-tenths of a mile after the first, and you should again be certain it is closed after going through.

From that point, all the way to the little mountain, excellent specimens of agate and chalcedony can be found scattered all over. Most of what can be procured is somewhat small, but the quality more than makes up for that minor deficiency. The prizes here are delicate pink banded agates which can be used to make incredibly beautiful cabochons. In addition, numerous well formed chalcedony roses can be picked up, some of which are quite sizeable. Occasionally the roses are covered with tiny quartz crystals and such pieces are great for display in a mineral collection. Sporadic geode-like, crystal filled chalcedony can also be obtained, but such specimens are few and far between.

It doesn't take long to gather quite a quantity of fine minerals at this site, but be advised that it is very remote and extra supplies should be carried in the event you are delayed.

"Antique pink" agate

AGATES AND GEODES

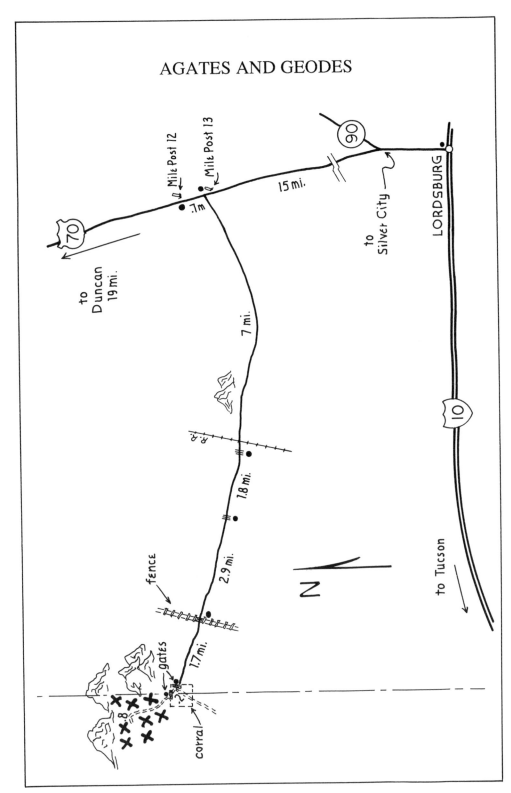

FIRE AGATE
Joy Valley

At one time, this well respected chalcedony and fire agate location was maintained by the B.L.M. for the exclusive use of rockhounds. The B.L.M. has recently given up that responsibility, however, due to the remote location, the expense of maintaining the road, and the limited number of visitors each year. The site remains open, though, and is still very productive.

To get there from Bowie, go north on Central Avenue one and eight-tenths miles and turn right onto Fan Road. From there, follow the instructions of the map another twenty one and seven-tenths miles to the base of the hills. The road is not bad, and most rugged vehicles should have no problem getting all the way.

The collecting area is extensive, covering many acres. There is a loop road which takes you near the mountains and chalcedony, some of which contains spectacular areas of fire, can be found by stopping just about anywhere along that road. As at other fire agate locations, there is beautiful material all over, much of which has the brown coloration denoting its potential for containing fire. The best pieces tend to be found nearer the mountains, away from the road. It seems that most people who collect here do what is easiest and search close to their vehicles, making distant spots more productive. Generally, the terrain is relatively flat, providing some great places for a dry camp.

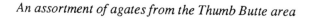

An assortment of agates from the Thumb Butte area

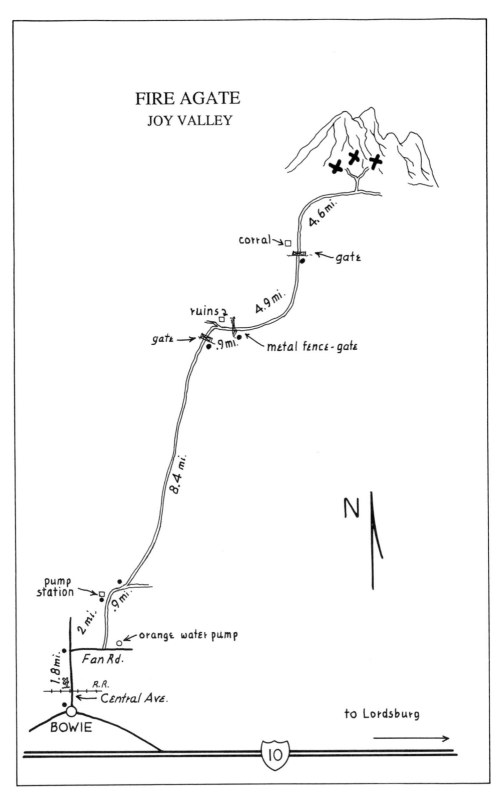

FIRE AGATE
JOY VALLEY

corral → □ ┤ ← gate

4.6 mi.

4.9 mi.

ruins? □ ┤
gate → ┤ ↖ metal fence-gate
.9 mi.

8.4 mi.

N ↑

pump
station → □
.9 mi.
2 mi.
○ orange water pump
Fan Rd.

1.8 mi.
R.R.
← Central Ave.

BOWIE

to Lordsburg →

10

115

MINERALS-TURQUOISE-GEODES
Gleeson Area

This is an interesting area and it will probably take more than one day to adequately explore all collecting opportunities offered. The mountains near Courtland, Gleeson and Pearce, as illustrated on the map, are littered with old mine dumps, many of which are abandoned and offer rockhounds opportunities for finding a variety of minerals including wulfenite, aurichalcite, pyrite, bornite, chrysocolla and rosasite. In fact, some of the finest bornite (peacock ore) to be found anywhere can be procured in the dumps just north of Gleeson.

Near Courtland is a turquoise mine which was operated by Tiffany's in the 1880's. The material found there was   beautiful and the mine is still operated sporadically. If interested in visiting this once prosperous prospect, an inquiry at the Pearce store may provide information in regard to current status.

Another area of interest is Sugar Loaf Mountain, near the road to Elfrida. Hunt for agate, green quartz, geodes and crystal filled geode pieces along the southern slopes.

Be careful when exploring abandoned mine dumps, since the associated terrain is often filled with hidden pits, shafts, rusty nails and broken glass. In addition NEVER enter a tunnel in this mining district. Many are flooded and the rock is rotten. Be also advised that there is still some mining being conducted in the locality, so DO NOT TRESPASS onto any privately owned dumps.

A good place from which to base.your exploration of this once rich mining district is in Tombstone, where there are campgrounds and motels.

The ghost town at Gleeson

GLEESON AREA

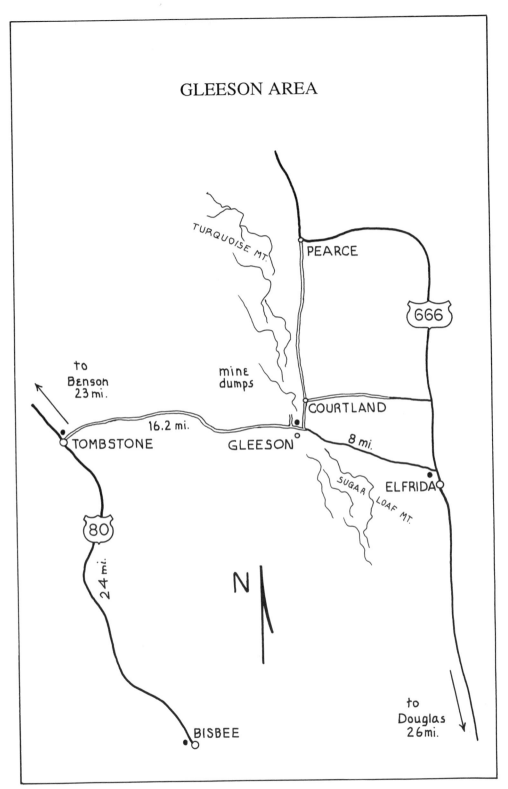

TURQUOISE MT.

PEARCE

666

mine
dumps

to
Benson
23 mi.

COURTLAND

16.2 mi.

TOMBSTONE

GLEESON

8 mi.

SUGAR LOAF MT.

ELFRIDA

80

24 mi.

N

to
Douglas
26 mi.

BISBEE

SELENITE ROSES
St. David Area

This is an easy area to reach, and features interesting selenite balls, as well as a host of other desirable minerals, including a colorful variety of banded rhyolite.

To get there from Benson, take Highway 80 four and nine-tenths miles south from town to Apache Powder Plant Road, which intersects from the right just as the highway curves to the left. Follow Apache Powder Plant Road three and one-half miles and turn right onto the ruts which weave toward the conspicuous flat-top hills about one and one-tenth miles away. This last stretch is sandy in spots, but rugged vehicles should have no problems.

Park anywhere near the hills and randomly explore them. The rhyolite is easy to see, being very colorful, but the selenite is much the same hue as the surrounding soil, making it more difficult to spot. Generally, the selenite is found in the red-brown regions and digging into the soft soil is necessary in order to find the choicest pieces. You should be able to find lots of small selenite roses and stars, but sizeable ones are more rare. Be careful when digging, since the selenite is very fragile when first exposed to the air.

The hills are quite extensive, and it would probably be worthwhile to explore as large a portion as possible. Sections of the hills situated further from the access roads will tend to be less picked over and thereby offer better potential for finding a greater supply of quality material.

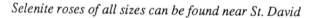

Selenite roses of all sizes can be found near St. David

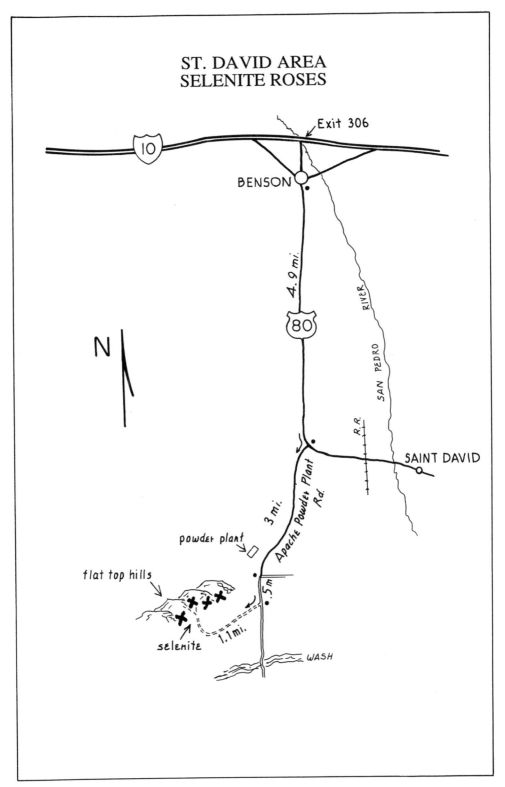

ST. DAVID AREA
SELENITE ROSES

Exit 306

10

BENSON

4.9 mi.

80

N

SAN PEDRO RIVER

R.R.

SAINT DAVID

3 mi.

Apache Powder Plant Rd.

powder plant

flat top hills

.5 m

selenite

1.1 mi.

WASH

PATAGONIA MINING AREA

This is a great place to spend some time. The region offers pleasant scenery, as well as a host of mineral collecting opportunities. All major roads are fairly good, and should not present a problem to most vehicles, if driven carefully.

Lots of copper was found in the region and associated ores including colorful chrysocolla, malachite and bornite can be found on numerous dumps. In addition, near Washington Camp, specimens filled with glistening pyrite are not uncommon, some in combination with vivid green epidote and quartz.

The dumps at Duquesne also boast cubic crystals of pyrite, as well as malachite, calcite and quartz crystals. The Nash Mine also provides pyrite and other minerals, and the main road runs right through the middle of the dump.

The accompanying map provides a general overview of the region. Much of the mineral crystallization is concealed within the host rock, requiring suspect stones to be split in order to properly ascertain what might be hidden inside. Be sure to wear goggles if you do crack rocks. In addition, be advised that the ownership status of these mines changes from time to time. A dump that was open to collectors yesterday might now be closed, and vice versa. Always ascertain current collecting status BEFORE trespassing. In addition DO NOT EVER ENTER ANY SHAFTS. Some are very unstable, and could collapse at the slightest provocation.

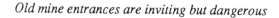

Old mine entrances are inviting but dangerous

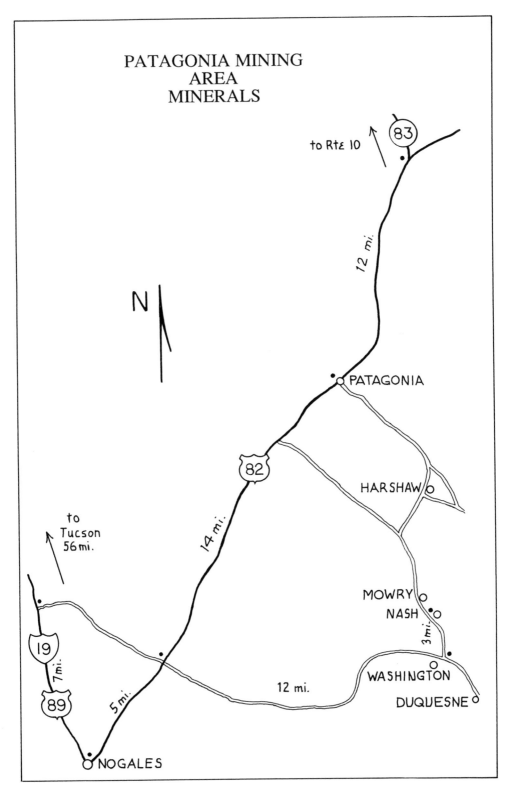

PATAGONIA MINING
AREA
MINERALS

to Rte 10

83

12 mi.

N

PATAGONIA

82

HARSHAW

14 mi.

to
Tucson
56 mi.

MOWRY
NASH

3 mi.

19

7 mi.

WASHINGTON

12 mi.

DUQUESNE

89

5 mi.

NOGALES

Gemstone and Mineral Locator

Gemstone and Mineral Locator